TRACES OF THE TRINITY

Signs of God in Creation and Human Experience

Peter J. Leithart

BrazosPress
a division of Baker Publishing Group
Grand Rapids, Michigan

© 2015 by Peter J. Leithart

Published by Brazos Press
a division of Baker Publishing Group
P.O. Box 6287, Grand Rapids, MI 49516-6287
www.brazospress.com

Printed in the United States of America

Library of Congress Cataloging-in-Publication Data is on file at the Library of Congress, Washington, DC.

ISBN 978-1-58743-367-2

15   16   17   18   19   20   21   7   6   5   4   3   2   1

To Elliot Paige Leithart

While *Traces of the Trinity* was going through the editorial process, my son Sheffield and his wife, Laura, opened their home to their first child, a daughter, Elliot Paige. I complete the book with the prayer that the Spirit of Jesus will forever make his home in Elliot, as he already has, and that she will find a permanent dwelling place in Jesus her Lord. May the Spirit enlarge her, so she will be capacious for her parents, for her future siblings and spouse and children, and for many, many friends. Elliot and I have not yet met, but I trust that the Spirit is already preparing a place in her heart for me, as he has made room in my heart for her.

Contents

Preface   vii

1. Outside In, Inside Out   1
2. Like Father, Like Son   17
3. I Am His, He Is Mine   35
4. Presence of the Past   49
5. Word in Word in World   63
6. Chords   83
7. Making Room   97
8. The Supple Imagination   113
9. I in Thee, Thou in Me   129

Postscript   147
Notes   155

Preface

Godly speculation can have an edifying function.
—John Frame

This is a book of theological speculation. The particular form of speculation has a long pedigree in Christian theology, present in seminal form already in Augustine and the Cappadocians and developed through the centuries under the heading of *vestigia Trinitatis*, which might be translated as "traces of the Trinity." The aim is to discover and lay bare echoes, vestiges, traces, clues to trinitarian life within the creation.[1] This tradition has fallen on hard times in some circles of late, for reasons I explore briefly in the postscript. I think that unfortunate, and hope that this essay will contribute to a revival of this neglected area of theological speculation.

My goal is, more specifically, to point to the traces of what theologians call "perichoresis" in creation and in human experience. Perichoresis means "mutual indwelling," or "reciprocal penetration," and describes the exhaustive mutual indwelling of the persons of the Trinity, the mystery of the Father's being in

vii

the Son that is eternally simultaneous with the Son's indwelling of the Father, and their mutual dwelling in the Spirit.

What I offer is not *doctrinal* speculation. Nothing I say here violates any point of trinitarian dogma, and, unlike some other writers who have written on perichoresis,[2] I make no suggestions for "revising" or "enhancing," much less for "correcting," trinitarian orthodoxy. I'm not opposed in principle to such efforts. We still have much to learn about the Triune God from Scripture. But that is not my aim in this essay. Instead of doctrinal speculation, I seek to extend trinitarian categories and patterns of thought to creation. This is an exercise in trinitarian "worldview."

The traces I discuss are of different kinds. Sometimes (as in chapters 1, 3, 6, and 7), I describe concrete physical traces of perichoresis. At other times, the mutual indwelling is more psychological or emotional (chapter 2), and at still other times it is conceptual (chapters 4, 5, and 8). In many chapters, I move from one mode to another, from physical to psychological to conceptual and back. I realize that some of the analogies I examine are clearer and more convincing than others. I realize too that I have not written an exhaustive study of the perichoretic features of creation. My speculations are suggestive, not definitive. In fact, my aim is not first of all to convince the readers of my specific conclusions, though I would like to do that. My first aim is to shape the way my readers think about and respond to the world around them, even to re-form the shape of their thought. I want to convince readers who are used to thinking in straight lines and sharp angles of the virtues of thinking in chiasms, spirals, curves, coils, twists, swirls, and whorls. If I do no more than leave my readers in a state of enhanced alertness, if I leave them anticipating that traces of triune life will meet them under every stone and in every sunset and in the face of every stranger, I will be satisfied.

The organization of the book requires a brief explanation. In form, it might be mistaken for a piece of natural theology, a nontheological foundation for revealed theology. For eight chapters I talk about creation—the relation of human beings to the world and to one another, sex, time, language, music, ethics, and logic—and finally, in the ninth chapter, I come to talk about the Trinity. The book seems to use the notion of *vestigia Trinitatis* in just the way Barth forbade: it might appear that I claim to arrive at trinitarian conclusions without having to go to the trouble of believing the gospel or reading Scripture.

The reality is the opposite. My starting point is the biblical and redemptive-historical revelation of the Trinity, along with the dogmatic and doctrinal tradition of trinitarian theology, and, assisted by a number of recent theologians,[3] I attempt to discern how trinitarian theology illuminates the world we live in. My opening assumption is simple-minded: Christians believe that the Triune God created the world, and that should have *some* implications for the kind of world that it is. Many Christians have acknowledged the perichoretic shape of the life of the Trinity, and that in particular should leave some trace in the world that has been made and remade by the Father, Son, and Spirit. Instead of working up to the Trinity from creation, this book looks *through* the doctrine of the Trinity to see if it illumines the way the world is. I believe it does, and I hope the results are edifying.

Outside In, Inside Out

lance around the place where you are reading. What's there? Many things, I expect—unless, perchance, you're reading this in an empty, white (padded?) room, which I hope you aren't.

Surrounding *me* are computer, desk, lamp, printer, unkempt piles of books, a loveseat and an old rocker, and the recliner to which I will shortly repair for a well-deserved afternoon nap. I hear my daughter practicing piano in the next room and the exhausted huffing and puffing of my nearly dead space heater. I smell the dust I stirred up packing boxes earlier today, and I can feel the keyboard and desktop and taste the bitter black coffee that is life's elixir.

And at the center of everything is the thing I experience most immediately: me. Me doing the viewing and the hearing and the smelling and the tasting and the touching and the typing. Me also presumably doing whatever thinking is going into this paragraph, and the previous one and the next. To other people, I'm one of the outside things, just as they are outside things to me.

When my daughter enters the room to ask if she can invite her friend over, she joins the table and the floor and the coffee mugs I keep for students as one more object in the room. My daughter is a different *sort* of object from the others. I have to drink a lot of coffee before my mug asks if he can ask *his* friend over. It might feel like my recliner is hugging me as I drift off to sleep, but that's just overactive imagination or overconsumption of coffee. My daughter, though, she hugs me, though not always voluntarily.

It's a complicated world, stuffed with stuff, but we find it easy to simplify, to whittle down the welter of bloomin' buzzin' confusion to two patches on the map: Outside there's the world with its things and its beauties with their aromas and sounds and tastes. Inside is me, my mind, the sensing thinking feeling thing. There's the world of objects, and there's me the subject, my skin forming a clear boundary between the two. It's Me versus World.

A skeptic might say that this seems easy only because I have been schooled in the misleading metaphysics of modernity. Only since René Descartes, one might say, have people chopped up the world this way. Descartes lived in a time of religious conflict. For centuries before, the Catholic Church had so dominated the intellectual and imaginative life of Europe that Christianity was all but taken for granted. In Descartes's day, one could no longer accept what the church said because now you had to ask the question, *Which* church? Some were beginning to say, None of them! But what then? Perhaps we can never know the truth about anything. Descartes didn't like the prospect of being doomed to ignorance, but if he wanted certainty—which he certainly did—he had to bypass religion and find a back way in.

The back door to certainty was labeled "Doubt." Descartes doubted the existence of the objects that surrounded him, the waxy candle burning away in his darkening room, his memories of the past, the traditions he had inherited. After all, he could not be absolutely certain that his experience of seeing the candle was real. We have all heard things that weren't there, seen things that turned out to be mirages, and René Descartes had had those sorts of experiences too. He might be dreaming. Or his experience might be the work of a very clever, very powerful demon, who had snuck into the room to derail the course of modern philosophy before it began. One cannot be too careful.

But when it was all whittled away, when he had cut away all the doubtful chaff from what was there, he could still be certain of one thing: *himself.* Suppose he's dreaming—but *he's* doing the dreaming. Suppose he is deceived—but *he* must exist to be deceived if he is being deceived. Even the evil demon's deceptions could be turned into proofs of his own existence.

But Descartes wanted to be more specific. The "me" that he discovered inside had a particular form and character. The only thing he knew for certain was that the "me" that was dreaming or being deceived or doubting was *thinking.* The thing he discovered, the thing he knew with absolute certainty, was that there existed in him a thinking thing. The world outside Descartes, including his own body, was a material machine, objects made of inert atoms, chugging along according to predictable, scientific laws. Inside was a thinking thing. It was subject versus object, René versus the World. One philosopher, Gilbert Ryle, unkindly called it the "ghost in the machine."

Cogito, ergo sum, Descartes cried. The stars flickered, the seas shifted restlessly, and the gears of the universe groaned as the world became modern.

Well, maybe not quite like that, but Descartes *did* open up a new way of thinking about the world and the self, about the inside me and the world of objects outside me. He created a modern version of "mind-body dualism." He imagined a world, the skeptic would say, in which it was natural to think of the world of objects out there and me in here. This picture has come to be so obvious to us that it's hard to conceive of anything else. I have some sympathy with the skeptic, for reasons I will explore below. Still, you *can*, if you like, divide everything into you-and-everything-else. Even when my daughter hugs me tightly, she is still herself. When I drift to sleep in my favorite chair, chair and man don't become a single blended entity, call it a "chan" or a "mair." My digestive system is a machine for turning coffee into alert parts of me, but while it's waiting in the cup or slipping down my throat the coffee is coffee. Things are different, irreducibly so. Nothing is other than itself.

Once you've made those distinctions, though, you've understood at best half of the pattern of things, and arguably it's not the most interesting half. The world is divided into things, but those things group together in all sorts of ways, forming complex patterns and shifting networks and intricate relationships with one another. I own my chair. I look at it fondly, even longingly, as the afternoon wears wearily on. Sometimes I sit in my chair, sometimes leaning back for that well-deserved nap I mentioned earlier. I have economic, physical, emotional, and other sorts of attachments to my chair—and even more so to my daughter.

I am different from the things around me, yet I'm also inseparably intertwined with them. The world isn't just outside; it's also inside. I'm not only outside the rest of the world; I'm in it. My connection with the world is a Celtic knot. Inside and outside form a Möbius strip that folds back on itself.

That may sound strange and mystical, but it's not hard to see. Let's start simply. Consider the obvious fact that you have a body. Descartes knew he had a body, but he believed his body was part of the external world that lay outside his real self, his thinking mind.[1] His body was the closest bit of that extension he called space. It was the machine nearest to his mind.

But this doesn't describe how we actually experience our bodies. If my hand got mangled in an industrial accident, it would be absurd for me to tell sympathetic friends, "Oh, it's fine. After all, the accident only happened to my *hand*, not to *me*." If I said that, my friends would wonder if my brain had also gotten mangled in the process. What the apostle Paul said about the church as the body of Christ is a truism for all bodies: when one member suffers, all suffer; when one member rejoices, all rejoice. Each member is a member for and of the whole. You can't detach one part of you from the other and identify one or the other as the "real me." We are mind-body unities, and my body is as much me as my mind is. Pain would be concentrated in my hand, but my entire body, including of course my brain, would be entirely involved in the event.

Once we recognize that—and we have to be trained *not* to recognize it—we can see that we aren't sitting outside the world peering in. We *inhabit* the world. Since we have bodies and *are* bodies, we occupy space in the world. We bump into things, rest our elbows on the table, tap on the keyboard with our fingers. The world bumps us back, taps us in turn, and our life takes shape in the sometimes clumsy dance that goes on between me and my environment. The French philosopher Maurice Merleau-Ponty put it well: "The body is the vehicle of being in the world, and to have a body is, for a living creature, to be involved in a definite environment, to identify oneself with certain projects and be continually committed to them."[2]

This isn't just about our bodies and their actions either. Merleau-Ponty got it right again: "Truth does not 'inhabit' only the 'inner man.'" Truth inhabits the body too. Then Merleau-Ponty went on, more radically, to say, "more accurately, there is no inner man" because "man is in the world, and only in the world does he know himself."[3]

You are in the world. *You* are in the world, not merely some heavy attachment called "body." The window we're trying to peer through is opaque, but a beam of light is shining through. It's enough to keep us going.

Not only are you in the world, but there is also a continuous interchange between your body and the world. The skin that seems to be such a clear boundary between inside and outside is permeable. Human beings have about five million hairs, each of them with a pore. As late as the 1960s, many believed that oxygen exchanges take place through our pores, that we inhale and exhale through the skin, and if our skin gets blocked, we suffocate. In Ian Fleming's *Goldfinger*, an unfortunate girl suffocates when she is painted head to foot in gold. The filmmakers, intent on keeping their actress alive (for publicity reasons, perhaps), left a patch of her skin exposed so that oxygen exchanges could continue.

Oxygen exchanges through the skin are a myth, but some creatures do breath through their skin—some species of earthworms and some amphibians. Even one mammal, the marsupial mouse, takes in oxygen through its pores. If air doesn't enter their skin, if air doesn't exit later, they will die. So, a warning: don't paint a marsupial mouse with gold paint.

Our pores need to be kept open too, though not for oxygen exchanges. If our skin is blocked, we break out with pimples and blackheads, and that can be mighty unpleasant. Much to our embarrassment, and to the delight of antiperspirant and cosmetic manufacturers, icky sticky often stinky stuff oozes out of us all the time. But that sweat keeps us alive. People suffering from anhidrosis don't have the automatic body-coolant mechanism the rest of us have, and they are at greater risk of dying from heat exhaustion.

Our skin has pores; it is porous. Because it is, so are we.

You have to look closely to see your pores, but our bodies are pocked with larger holes, just as essential to life. You might have noticed. If not, take a look in the mirror and count the holes in your head alone, and then work your way modestly down your body. You'll find a couple more holes lower down. The upper holes let outside things inside. The lower holes force what's inside back outside. We are porous because we have gigantic pores that we call mouth, nostrils, ears, eyes, urethra, and anus. Roughly half of us humans have vaginas that open up into a uterus, everyone's first home.

We can live with our skin pores covered, but we cannot live if our giant holes get blocked. We breathe seven to eight liters of air per minute, which amounts to about four hundred cubic feet a day, 550 liters being oxygen. That's a lot of the outside to welcome in every day, but it needs to be done. Cut off the flow of oxygen from outside into your lungs for more than a few minutes, and you die.

Americans drink around a gallon of water a day, half from drinks other than water and about one-fifth from the food we eat. We can survive longer without water than without oxygen— about five days—but when we're deprived of water, our cells lose fluids that are necessary for the cells to function properly. We need water to have bodies at all, since more than half of our body weight is water. For infants just from the womb, the proportion is even higher, close to three-quarters of the baby's weight. Without water, we die.

And of course we need food. Food comes in all enticing styles and delectable flavors. It's far more than fuel, but it is fuel. Mahatma Gandhi reportedly survived twenty-one days without food and with only a few sips of water.[4] Hunger strikes have gone on longer, up to forty days. At Mount Sinai, Moses fasted forty days, as did Jesus in the wilderness at the beginning of his ministry. Most of us have trouble functioning well more than a few hours without a meal. Women need about 2,000 calories a day. Men have it better: nutritionists recommend a daily intake of 2,500 calories for bulkier males.

Once we've eaten food and our digestive system has squeezed all the nutrients from it, we need to return the remainder to the world through our anus. A few years ago, Elvis Presley's physician, George Nichopoulos, revealed that the King might have died of chronic constipation. At death, his colon was twice its normal diameter and twice its normal length. An autopsy revealed that the stool in his intestines had been there for four or five months when he died. If a human doesn't have a bowel movement in a week, it can lead to sepsis and death. Urine has to be expelled more regularly. It is sometimes possible to go a day and a half without urinating, but if the bladder gets too full and is not emptied, the urine backs up into the kidneys, and this can have serious health results.

We humans don't live long unless the world goes in and out on a regular—momentary, daily—basis. We don't live *well* unless other things enter through our pores. What would life be without Beethoven's *String Quartets* or Handel's *Messiah*? What would life be if you could never hear the voice of your mother, your lover, your spouse, your toddler? Impoverished for sure, even dangerous: if you were deaf, you couldn't hear the elephant crashing toward you through the bush, the burglar sneaking into the house in the dead of night, the ominous footsteps behind you in a dark street. Those transporting, and welcoming, and warning sounds enter our bodies by vibrating the air until it reaches our eardrum. If the vibrating world didn't come into us from outside, we'd live in a world of utter silence.

And utter darkness. According to the current theory of vision,[5] light rays bounce off the things outside us and enter our eyes through the cornea, which refracts the rays through the pupil. Controlled by the iris, the light passes to the lens, which flexes and bends to focus the rays on the retina at the back of your eyeball. The rods and cones on your retina detect the colors of the light and the details of what you have seen, and the cells of the retina turn the light into electrical impulses that are sent along the optic nerve to the brain, where an image is somehow produced. The process seems instantaneous, and it fools us into forgetting that we are taking the world in every time we glance around us. Our ability to see depends on part of the world—light, whatever that is—entering into our bodies and being transformed into the sort of impulses that our brains can "read." Unless the world enters us, we're blind.

Whenever I smell boxwoods, I am instantly transported back to my youth, exploring the cobbled streets and colonial homes of Williamsburg, Virginia, with my family. Smell is as physical as any of the other senses. Diane Ackerman notes,

> When I hold a violet to my nose and inhale, odor molecules float back into the nasal cavity behind the bridge of the nose, where they are absorbed by the mucosa containing receptor cells bearing microscopic hairs called cilia. Five million of these cells fire impulses to the brain's olfactory bulb or smell center. Such cells are unique to the nose. . . . The neurons in the nose are replaced about every thirty days and, unlike other neurons in the body, they stick right out and wave in the air current like anemones on a coral reef.[6]

What would life be like if you never smelled a rose, or your wife's favorite perfume wafting across the room before you see her enter, or the warm musk of a child's hair? Impoverished. But what would life be like if you didn't smell the rancid butter or the sour milk, or the natural gas leaking into the room? Life might well be nasty, and might even be short. We need to smell, and we want to experience the pleasures of smell, but we won't unless the world breaks through the shell of our outside into our inside.

We don't live richly unless we take the outside world in, but this is not just a "quality of life" issue. The point is more fundamental. We don't have any experience of living in the world *at all* unless the world lives in us. We know that we exist when sound waves on the air strike our inner ear, when our eyes receive light reflected from objects outside, when our noses receive the molecules that carry odor to those sensitive nerves. When we die and no longer take the world into ourselves, our corpses are still lumps of flesh in the world. But lumps of flesh don't have any *experience* of existing in the world. To experience being in the world, the world has to enter.

Imagine yourself in a room without light and sound, and imagine that torturers have somehow also removed all aromas and tastes. Imagine too that you have lost all sense of touch, so that you can't feel the walls of your prison. It's a terrifying picture, because it's very close to death. Experience as such, experience as we know it, is experience of being in the world. If we eliminate all the inputs from the world, we wouldn't merely cease to experience the world. We'd stop experiencing. Even Helen Keller could feel the water trickling over her fingers and the vibrations of her teacher's vocal chords.

It's not only the stuff in the world that enters me as I inter-act with it. The arrangement of things in space and in places I enter also enters me. I don't experience individual objects individually, discretely. I experience them in ensembles—the lamp and computer on the desk; the window looking out over the computer screen; the houses of the neighborhood and, very very occasionally, a living, breathing neighbor; the trees down by the Cahaba River beyond the houses. But I can't inhabit this place unless the place also comes to inhabit me. Without that cohabitation, I have no experience of being in that place at all. Besides, I carry around the places of my past life in me, and they can capture me unbidden. New places that inhabit me evoke old places I used to inhabit. Out in the Alabama woods for a "winter" walk or passing the snowy woodlands around Chicago, I am thrown back into my past. I'm eleven again, crossing frozen Big Walnut Creek to climb the slippery, steep, tree-tangled hill on the far side.

Descartes notwithstanding, knowledge, including self-knowledge, doesn't come abubblin' up from within. If it does, it's likely to be false or at least limited. Even at the most elementary level, we learn by taking the world in. We discover that lilacs are purple and aromatic because we see and smell them. But we don't know they're "aromatic" unless we've learned what that word means, and we learned that from another English-speaking person. As many have pointed out, Descartes himself couldn't forget everything. If he wanted to publish his theory—and he did—he had to remember Latin or French and how to write. He had to believe that the French or Latin he wrote would be understood by his readers. Doubt can only go so far.

No English speaker invented the English language, any more than Descartes invented the French and Latin in which he wrote his treatises. We entered into a world where the English language already existed, and I imagine that many of the readers of this book entered a world where parents and siblings already spoke English, and through a variety of different avenues we put two and two together, to distinguish *two* from *to* from *too*, and began to master English. This all comes to us from elsewhere. We didn't make it up in our heads. Any language we might be able to make up would be incapable of doing what languages do, which is to communicate with other people. Our teachers, our traditions, our learned habits and accumulated factoids and ideas are not obstacles to knowledge, as Descartes suggested. They are the very stuff of knowledge. Without them, we probably couldn't think at all, and we certainly couldn't converse or report or get feedback and correction.

We do produce ideas from within. We can take *this* and combine it with *that*, stir together this insight and that observation, mix this book and that event in creative ways. We can think logically through a series of axioms to arrive at reliable conclusions. All of these mental operations, though, depend on having our minds fat and healthy with nutrition from without. Our brains, like our mouths and bellies, feed on the world. Learning is feasting, a taking-in of the world so that it becomes us, coursing through our brains the way nutrients flow through our blood.

If we don't retain things we've learned, life will be a constant tumble. Every time we walk through the house, we'll bump into chairs and sofas whose location we've forgotten. Every time we meet someone, we'll have to be reintroduced. But forgetting is essential to a properly functioning mind too. If we remembered every last thing we had ever done or said, the weight of memory would be crushing. Some of our neurons actually enable us to forget, so that we can move on from what has happened.[7] Our thoughts don't empty out into the world the way urine does, but many things that come into the mind leave the mind for parts unknown. The mind lives as much by a respiratory rhythm of inhalation and exhalation as our lungs. Our minds as well as our bodies have to excrete.

The world that surrounds us comes into us, so that we surround parts of it. What envelops us becomes enveloped by us. It's not René versus the Universe, Me versus the World. That apparently thick wall that separates subject from object, inside from outside, is full of passageways, and the two only exist as distinct realities because of exchanges across the boundary, only because the *out* comes *in* and the *in* goes *out*. I am in the world, and the world is in me, and I exist only because both are true.

Solid as they appear, the objects outside of me aren't any more self-enclosed than I am. Since the birth of modern physics and chemistry, we've known that most of the space of a "solid" object is empty. Ernest Rutherford discovered in 1909 that when he shot a beam of alpha rays at a sheet of gold foil, most of the rays simply went through the sheet, leading him to the then-revolutionary, now-elementary conclusion that objects are mostly empty space. Radiologists beam X-rays through your body and other objects. Objects are porous too.

And they're porous all the way down to the subatomic level. Atoms aren't what Newton believed they were, "solid, massy, hard, impenetrable, movable particles." They are more like "structures of activity, patterns of energetic vibration within fields."[8] Things made up of porous atoms are themselves porous. Mass itself is not really massive either. According to the current model of particle physics, "The mass of a particle like an electron or proton is not inherent in the particle itself but depends on its interaction with a field called a Higgs field," where the particles interact with theoretical Higgs bosons.[9] As Karl Popper puts it, "Matter turns out to be highly packed energy, transformable into other forms of energy; and therefore something in the nature of a process."[10] Objects feel solid not because they are packed tight with protons and neutrons, but because of the electrical forces of protons and electrons. The electrons of a table repel the electrons of my hand with such force that I can't push my hand through the empty space.[11]

The world comes into me and makes me what I am, a living, experiencing person. But the effect goes the other direction too. I'm not in the world merely as an object on the outside of all other objects. When I'm around, my presence affects the world around me. Irreducibly distinct as I am, I am truly *in* the world. I indwell not only the environment in general but also specific objects in my environment.

Robert Hughes offers a charming example. Mice go about their business whether we perceive them or not. But when we are present, our sheer presence changes the way a mouse behaves. It remains a mouse, but it is a mouse in a particular mode because of my presence in the room. By the same token, if I happen to encounter the mouse, my experience and reaction to it will be colored by what I know about mice from previous encounters, storybooks I read as a child, what I think are the scientific facts about mice. Whether I bend down to stroke it with my index finger or leap onto a chair is determined by these personal factors. If the mouse were not in the room, I would neither bend down nor leap into the chair. My behavior depends on the presence of a small, cute—or scary—mammal in the room. As Hughes summarizes, "Reality . . . is interaction."[12]

I'm not just an external object to the mouse. When I'm there, I change the mouse "on the inside."

Well, of course, we say: the mouse reacts to me because it's alive and it senses me in the same way I sense it.

But it's not only living things that are affected by me. Early in the twentieth century, physicists, those most rigorously mathematical and logical of the tribe of scientists, began to notice the disquieting fact that the presence of an observer affects the behavior of the things observed. Earlier scientists thought "they could formulate their science without any reference, even an implicit one, to the states of consciousness of observers," but they have come to recognize that "the principles of physics cannot even be formulated without referring . . . to the impressions—and thus the minds—of the observers."[13] Those hard-looking objects out there are vulnerable to our presence and our observations.[14]

Descartes treated humans as detached spectators of the outside world. But unless we are philosophers, we don't have the luxury to be spectators. We don't first look over the world as a set of objects and patterns to analyze and classify. We engage the world as a set of objects that already have particular meanings and uses for us. The philosopher Martin Heidegger put it this way: The world is not "present at hand," waiting to be analyzed and thought about. It's "ready to hand," full of items that have their own shapes, purposes, uses, histories.[15]

Heidegger fancied himself a peasant, and a lot of his examples are homely, peasantish examples. A hammer isn't just a piece of wood with a shaped piece of metal at the top. It is more than its material qualities. It is a *tool*, useful for driving nails, not useful for sawing clean lines. The hammer is what it is because of how human beings use it. It is not an object "outside" of me; it's defined by the uses I make of it. It is "ready-to-hand," designed for me to use it. When I pick it up, it becomes an extension of me. When I'm using it, the hammer isn't an object "out there."

The offending, protruding nail is my enemy, and my hammer and I work together to defeat it.

We might think that we should distinguish between what the hammer is and what it is *to me*, but that doesn't work. If I've never seen a hammer before, if I don't know its proper use, if I pick it up and start to scratch my back with it, it's not merely that I don't know how to use the hammer properly. I don't even know what the thing *is* unless I know it as a hammer, as something to drive nails with. It's *not* a wood-and-metal thing; what it is in its "deepest essence" is what it is in its proper use, a hammer. And that means that I'm not just an observer of hammers, but I'm one of the beings that makes hammers be what hammers are. The thing *is* a hammer. That's its "essence," but it has that essence only because of human beings who make and use it. The hammer would not be a hammer—it would not be what it *is*—without us.

It's fairly easy to see that the boundary between me and the world is porous, and that it *has* to be so—physically, intellectually, metaphysically. It's a little harder to see that the pores open in both directions, that I make the world by dwelling in it as much as the world makes me by dwelling in me. It's even harder to see that objects in the world are what they are by indwelling *one another*. But that's the argument I want to make.

Go back to the beginning: Glance around the room. What's there? There's a collection of objects that can be distinguished from one another. The cup is not the coffee is not the table is not the lamp is not the computer screen. Yet together they form a little village of objects. Together they form an environment, and that environment determines what the objects are as much as the objects make up the environment. My cup is not the coffee, but if the cup never held coffee, and especially if it were *incapable* of holding coffee, it wouldn't be much of a coffee cup. The lamp is a lamp because it illumines the things I want to see on my desk. It's not the same as the things on my desk;

they don't mush together into an undifferentiated mass. But the lamp isn't much of a lamp without the other objects that it makes visible. The window in front of me is a window because of its particular properties—it's made of transparent glass and has metal and plastic frames to hold the glass in place. But it wouldn't be a window without the rest of the house. To be a window, it needs the wall and the light that passes through the window. The wall isn't the window, nor is the light, but without the wall and light, the window would not be a window.[16]

Things are defined not only in themselves but also by their relations with other things. One thing enters into the definition of another thing: "coffee" co-defines "coffee cup," and "wall and house" co-define "window." Things are so intimately "in" each other that you can't even describe the substance of one without reference to the others. Object defines object. Even while they remain irreducibly different, objects are what they are only because they exist in networks of relation to each other, so that one thing "curls back" to make another thing what it is. Things indwell things, and without this indwelling, nothing can be the particular thing it is. Nothing is other than what it is, but nothing is what it is except by the other things that dwell in it, the other things among which it dwells.

Offend my house, and you offend me.
(also because I own those things; Offend
God's people, and you offend him.

Like Father, Like Son

One is the loneliest number there will ever be. And lonely is "the saddest experience you'll ever know." Thus says Three Dog Night.

It's a widespread sadness. J. H. van den Berg goes so far as to suggest that "loneliness is the nucleus of psychiatry," the "central core of illness, no matter what [the patient's] illness may be." Some mental illnesses have physical or genetic causes, but van den Berg argues that mental illness is primarily spiritual or, in the older meaning of the term, "psychic," a disorder of soul. And many mental illnesses arise from simple loneliness: "If loneliness didn't exist, we could reasonably assume that psychiatric illnesses could not occur either."[1] Humans connect to other humans at so basic a level that when we disconnect, our own souls shatter into a thousand little pieces.

Loneliness is not the same as solitude. History is peppered with solitaries—Christian hermits escaping into the howling desert to meditate and memorize Scripture, Hindu sadhus, Muslim Sufis, Emily Dickinson, the Buddha. One may question the mental health of some of these (especially Dickinson), but for many we could say, "If this be madness, let us all be mad." To believers, the eccentricities of solitaries are divine eccentricities, the kind that end with the solitary honored as a god, not spread on a psychiatrist's couch. Religious solitaries are awesome; the lonely are pathetic.

Madness existed prior to modernity, but the prominence of psychiatry is a modern phenomenon. Psychiatry is the therapeutic science of modern society, mopping up the inevitable if unintended consequences of the social changes we call "modernization." Modernity liberates. Children no longer have to follow in the footsteps of their parents. A son can be a lawyer, even if his ancestors worked the same plot of land from time immemorial. A daughter can move to the city for school or a job, away from the home village. In the city, she dresses, coifs, even walks differently. Moderns question traditional ways of life. Comfortable old ways strain, groan, finally splinter under the pressure of the new, the ever new. Pathways are no longer set. We can't tell where we're going or what we're to do by remembering the way it's always been done. We have to make it up as we go along.

We don't want to give up that freedom, but it comes with a sizable price tag. Modern institutions disrupt networks of relationship and patterns of life that bind people to each other and to particular pathways of life. When brothers and sisters and sons and daughters move to the city, they can't take care of their aging parents and siblings. They send money home, but it's not the same. Global markets open up opportunities unknown to traditional societies, but competition can ruin the old ways. Growing cities have their own forms of community. Urban neighborhoods can replicate the ethnic homogeneity of the mother country or the countryside, or create their own new forms of cosmopolitan community. The neighborhood bar takes the place of the village square. For many, though, especially for newcomers, the city is a place of anonymity and loneliness. If an urban immigrant is going to have friends, he is going to have to find them for himself. They don't come ready-to-hand.

The great Russian Orthodox theologian Alexander Schmemann observed, as only an immigrant to the United States could:

> For years, people have rushed to America for an easier life, not realizing that deep down, life is much more difficult there. First of all, America is a country of great loneliness. Each one is alone with his own fate, under a huge sky, in the middle of a colossal country. Any culture, tradition, roots seem small there, but people strongly cling to them, knowing full well their illusory character. Secondly, this solitude in America demands from everyone an existential answer to the question, to be or not to be, and that requires effort. Hence so many personal crashes. In Europe anyone who falls, falls on some ground; in America he flies into an abyss. So much fear, such angst.[2]

Loneliness is a social and psychological burden, but the theorists of political economy treat loneliness as the natural state of humanity. Whatever psychic wholeness individuals lose to modernization, they gain in theoretical elevation.

For all their differences, the founders of modern political theory, John Locke and Thomas Hobbes, both believed that in the original state of human life, each human being was fundamentally an individual pursuing his individual interests. Hobbes said this produced a horrific war of all against all. "Every man is enemy to every man," and in a state of such total and all-consuming war, there can be no industry, no cultivation, navigation, building, knowledge, arts, letters, society—in short, no civilization. People tremble in continuous fear because of the ever-present "danger of violent death." It eventually dawns on these pugnacious brutes that they are safer if they band together into gangs, but others have the same idea. In place of a war of every man against every man, we have an equally violent war of band against band. There are "laws" in the state of nature, but that doesn't prevent life from being "solitary, poor, nasty, brutish, and short."[3]

Hobbes thought the fears of lonesome natural men have a saving grace. Fear of death, along with desire for comfort and hope for gain from labor, encourages men to seek peace. Fear can keep them at peace, so long as what they fear is fearsome enough to keep them in utter and abject awe. Only one thing overawes savages, and that is greater savagery, a sovereign power greater than any other. Petty natural violence is checked only by absolute artificial violence. In order to secure the peace, human beings are willing to "confer all their power and strength upon one man, or upon one assembly of men," which boils down the "plurality of voices" and wills in order to reduce them to "one will." Every man agrees to submit his will to the one will of the sovereign; each bends his own judgment to conform to the sovereign's. Individuals are authors of the sovereign's actions, because each has covenanted to "personate" himself in that sovereign. It's all rather magical: the very act of generating this monstrous Leviathan unifies. In creating Leviathan, the humans who have warred to the death suddenly act as one man.[4]

Like Hobbes, Locke imagines a state of nature in which human beings are equal, without rank or privileges, and without any involuntary relations of subordination.[5] Each has his own rights, and each has the right to defend his rights: "The execution of the law of nature is, in that state, put into every man's hands," and so "every man has a right to punish the offender, and be executioner of the law of nature."[6]

Lockean natural man is jollier than his Hobbesian neighbor. According to Locke, there are natural forms of social life, in marriage, family, and household (including servants), and, above all, in trade. These forms of interaction fall "short of political society," since they have "different ends, ties, and bounds."[7] But the natural forms of social life, especially trade, encourage natural humans to band together into political societies. Political order exists to preserve property and punish offenses against property. Since this power belongs originally to the property owners, political society can exist only if each member "hath quitted this natural power."[8] Whenever anyone consents to the social contract, he gives up his power to the "majority of the community." The origin of "any political society is nothing but the consent of any number of freemen capable of a majority to unite and incorporate such a society."[9]

Hobbes and Locke agree that political community is an artificial construct. Especially for Hobbes, humans are basically alone and only secondarily in society. Hobbes's state comes to "personate" the whole commonwealth, but that is only because each has agreed to subject himself to this "mortal god." Leviathan can establish himself by force, but it's also possible that men will "voluntarily" agree to submit, in what Hobbes calls a "political Commonwealth, or Commonwealth by Institution."

Economic theory is equally individualistic at its foundations. Economic agents are individual producers and consumers. So long as they do not infringe on the rights of other economic actors to do the same, individuals should be free to act however they please. Once society comes into existence, it exists to enable individuals to produce, trade, and consume more efficiently.[10]

How these individuals come to be in the first place is a large lacuna in early modern political and economic thought. How do these individuals learn the skills necessary to engage in trade? How are Hobbes's warring individuals and bands capable of making covenant if they don't already share a language? And if they already have a unified language, there must have been some ordered society prior to the covenant, a "natural" and not "artificial" political community. Hobbes's theory only makes sense if there is a political order prior to the formation of political order; it only makes sense if it's not a theory of the origins of political order, which is what it claims to be. That's what is technically called a "problem."

Hobbes had an answer to this dilemma: "Let us return again to the state of nature, and consider men as if but even now sprung out of the earth, and suddenly (like mushrooms) come to full maturity without all kind of engagement to each other."[11] It's an answer, but not a convincing one. I don't know about you, but no one I know sprang from the ground like a mushroom, or was formed in the dust like Adam, or leaped from the head of Zeus, or rose from the earth like Cadmus, ready to battle dragons and sow the ground with their teeth. Even the most convinced Darwinist doesn't believe his neighbor is a former crustacean who emerged from the ooze to grow into a primate.

Sociology was invented to correct the individualism of political theory and economics.[12] Sociologists take "society" as a basic fact, as *the* basic fact, prior to politics, culture, or religion, and prior to the goals and aspirations of individuals. Society is not something to be explained, but rather it *is* the explanation. Sometimes the explanation is crass: Republicans oppose Barack Obama and the Democrat agenda not because they sincerely want to protect American freedoms or to advance the common good, but simply because they share the interests of the upper middle class. Debunking of this sort is obviously reversible: the only reason Democrats think that Republicans act in the interests of their class is because they were raised in the blue states and graduated from tony Ivy League universities. A debate at this level is not, shall we say, altogether productive or edifying.[13]

That's a crude example, but sophisticated sociological models make similar assumptions about the causal power of "the social." Mary Douglas has developed a theory of society and religion based on two variables, which she describes as group and grid. Group is the amount of direct, face-to-face contact one has with members of a group. Grid is a measure of social differentiation. A small group, a tribe for instance, would be "high group," while a bureaucracy would be "low group." Militaries are "high grid," while a set of roommates is "low grid." From these factors, Douglas attempts to predict styles of religion, notions of virtue, ideas of the self, and art forms. Social factors—grid and group—explain other things.[14]

All this can be illuminating in various ways, but sociology doesn't really solve the problem of the individual and society. It simply flips it upside down. Instead of saying the individual is the fundamental unit, the building block out of which societies are made, sociology makes society the builder of individuals. For Hobbes, natural men sprang up like mushrooms in the shadow of a tree. For sociology, societies spring up magically like an exotic variety of social fungus.

In these theoretical shifts, one assumption remains constant— namely, that "individual" and "society" are separate enough that one can influence, mold, shape, or create the other. Individualists assume that individuals are similar to hard atoms of human nature capable of bumping into one another but not capable of indwelling one another. Sociologists assume that society is an entity that can be isolated from the individuals who make it up and from other factors like religion and morality. Sociologists assume that individuals are "outside of" and "external to" other individuals and to the groups around them, at least external enough so that society can bully individuals into doing its bidding.

This problem should sound familiar. Remember what we learned in chapter 1: Though I'm distinct from the world, I don't stand over against it as something outside of me. The world inhabits me even as I inhabit the world, and neither the world nor I could be what we are without each other. Irreducibly different as the world is from me, and I from the world, each has to indwell the other if either is going to exist at all.

The same Möbius twist resolves the dilemma of individualism versus society, political economy versus sociology. Individuals are utterly unique. No individual can be reduced to another, nor are individuals simply a sum or product of others who have influenced them. Yet I'm the unique me that I am only because of those others who have molded me. Without those particular social others, I'd be a different me, and without me they'd all be different thems. Society has to dwell within individuals, and individuals within society, if either is to exist. In short, what is true of my relation to the inanimate world around me is true in an even more profound way in my relationships with other persons. If I am in the world as the world is in me, we can believe that it's even more the case that my friends and family indwell me as I pour my soul into them. If I have a reciprocal relationship with the rock and the tree and the leaf, how much more with mother and father, sister and brother, wife and children?

Hobbes to the contrary, everyone I know started life in a pretty intimate "engagement" with another human whom the child eventually learned to call mother, and that intimate engagement with Mom was the product of prior intimate "society" between Mom and a man who might turn out to be "Dad."[15] We all began life indwelling another human. Contrary to some proabortion rhetoric, a fetus is never just a part of Mom. It's a different biological organism, with different DNA, fingerprints, dental patterns. But the fetus would not be what it is without Mom. In the third trimester, the baby's heart rate slows when Mom speaks. Before they are born, babies know Mom's voice and have begun to learn Mom's native language. Even in utero fetuses react to bright lights shone at them from outside, lick the placenta and uterus and probably taste the flavors of the foods that Mom shares with them, and seem to recognize Mom by smell.

It goes the other way too: Mom is definitely affected by the little stranger who makes a home in her belly. She feels queasy in the mornings, sometimes vomits, grows at an alarming rate, tires, and eventually begins to feel internal butterfly flutters, and soon after she feels kicks and pokes. Before the baby makes an appearance, Mom traces the curve of the butt, cringes at the elbow in her ribs, feels the baby's headstand pirouettes.

Life in utero is a life of mutual interaction. Before we're visible to the world, we're already in society. The fetus is literally inside Mom, but much of Mom goes into the fetus too. Without that mutual indwelling, there is no Mom and there is no fetus. Natural loneliness is an illusion. If there's one thing we're *not* at the beginning, it's by ourselves. The isolation from my first home in my mother is traumatic, and babies find that the best response to the trauma is to howl.

What's true about our origins remains true once we are separated from Mom. I didn't create my identity as a white American Protestant on my own. Much of it was handed to me, some I picked up over time, nearly all of it I picked up by engaging with an outside world. Humans are not naked beings stripped of all these identifying marks, fundamentally unaffected by society. The "thinking thing" that Descartes thought was his "ego" has no ethnic and national identity. It's a person whose public life and activities don't touch his real being, a privatized something lurking inside his body.[16] But that Cartesian self is a fantasy, like the Hobbesian natural man.

We are beings-in-society, or, as Heidegger puts it, "Beings-with." It is a gnostic heresy to assume that humanity is mainly a "spiritual Thing" that is somehow "misplaced" in the world.[17] Being in a place among other people is the original condition of human beings. Heidegger describes this with his famous image of "thrownness": We are thrown into a world we didn't make, a world we don't know, surrounded by strangers to whom we are in turn a newly emerged stranger. Before we begin to be an actor, before we adopt projects and set agendas for our lives, we are passive and dependent. Individuals never exist except as beings who indwell some particular social reality.[18] A "bare subject without a world" never exists. We begin among "those from whom, for the most part, [one does] not distinguish oneself—those among whom one is too," those others we encounter "environmentally," as much a part of the setting of our lives as the crib and pacifier and blanket.[19]

Our relations with these others are not contractual. I didn't negotiate to get myself born into a family in central Ohio; no bargaining made me the son of a physician and a piano teacher. I didn't contract out to be baptized a Lutheran. I ended up *there* and *with them* through no fault or virtue of my own. If my original and most fundamental social relations are not contractual, isn't that a clue that contract is not the basic model for social relations?

What I receive from others is not just my "objective" identity that I put on my mortgage applications or passport. The emotional tonality of my life also arises from the social world in which I live, the world that first indwelled me. Some dimensions of our emotional tonality may come from genetic inheritance, but a great deal of it comes from our family of origin and the emotional habits of that family. If your mother screeched while your father cowered passively, that dynamic molds your own emotional responses. If you grew up, as I did, in a stiff Midwestern home, where emotional demonstrativeness didn't need to be forbidden because it was never a temptation, where the dinner table conversation consisted of "Pass the butter, please" and the sound of munching, where "Not too bad" was a superlative—then you might end up something like me.

Physical experience growing up shapes emotional life. My family was not huggy. Physical demonstrations of affection were not prohibited, merely not done. Midwestern Lutherans didn't do such things. I determined before I had children of my own that I would be a more physically affectionate father than my father, but that had to be a conscious decision to override my emotional and physical instincts. Some physical experiences can be devastating. Victims of childhood sexual abuse are plagued by long-term shame expressed in depression, anxiety, eating disorders, and addictions of various kinds. Sometimes the victimization inverts and turns cruel, and the cruelty can turn into sociopathology. Victims victimize.

I didn't make myself a reserved, comparatively quiet, somewhat stiff adult. I made decisions and choices, but much of my emotional formation took place before I was aware formation was taking place. This happened because my family setting curved around to inhabit me, even as I was taking up my place in it.

Family systems counselors have observed that family members often adopt predictable roles in families plagued by addictions like alcoholism. One kid ends up being the family clown, and everyone else relies on his humor to break the gloom. Another family member takes on the role of scapegoat, bearing the blame and burden for the rest of the family. Another becomes the enabler, and another child is likely to assume the guise of a "lost child." Family members become "codependents," the life of each one shaped as he or she assumes a role in reaction to the addiction of the one family member.[20] Traits learned in a dysfunctional family don't get shed like snake skin when the children become adults.[21]

A few centuries ago, David Hume noticed how much our self-image owes to the way others regard us, and attributed it to the human capacity for "sympathy." Sympathy occurs through the combination of "the impression or consciousness of our own person" and "the idea of the sentiments or passions of others." Our self-conception, Hume thinks, is "of all our ideas the liveliest and closest to us," and the ideas and moods of another have an effect on us to the extent that these ideas or impressions are close to our own sense of self. The fusion of self-image and the regard of others has a powerful shaping effect on our character.[22]

We internalize the judgments of others upon us, especially the judgments of those others whose approval we seek.

> By our continual and earnest pursuit of a character, a name, a reputation in the world, we bring our own deportment and conduct frequently in review, and consider how they appear in the eyes of those who approach and regard us. This constant habit of surveying ourselves, as it were, in reflection, keeps alive all the sentiments of right and wrong, and begets, in noble natures, a certain reverence for themselves as well as others, which is the guardian of every virtue. . . . The minds of men are mirrors to one another, not only because they reflect each other's emotions, but also because those rays of passions, sentiments, and opinions may often be reverberated, and may decay away by insensible degrees.[23]

I see myself in the mirror of others. My self-image is in part patched together from the way *others* look at me.

Personal habits and quirks are also picked up from outside. My brothers and I noticed sometime in our youth that our father always said "Um" when he first answered the telephone. We joked riotously, as only preteen boys can. I find myself today doing precisely the same thing. When a student asks a question, I have to get the family "Um" out of the way before I begin an answer. I once caught a student counting up the number of "Ums" in a lecture. The total was embarrassingly high. I've continued the family tradition by passing on the trait to my own children. One of my sons says it so frequently that his sisters began to call him "Mr. Um."

One of the disquieting experiences of parenting is discovering yourself saying or doing to your children what your parents did and said to you. The same verbal corrections, the same derisive laughter, the same sorts of jokes and puns, sometimes— regrettably—the very same jokes and puns: this is where parents' instincts go if left unchecked. You can stop and do something different. But the sheer fact that you have to make a decision to stop and do something different says something about the formative power of parental example. "Like father, like son," we often say, and that is rarely a statement about physical resemblance. It's more often a statement about outlook, tone of voice, emotion, the stance we take in life. We pick up our selves from Mom and Dad.

And not just from Mom and Dad. My father was not a sports fan. He would occasionally sit with us to watch a football game, so long as the contestants were Ohio State and Michigan. In junior high, I became obsessed with sports. For the better part of a decade, basketball was my life. I watched games on television whenever I could, and then, inspired by Dr. J's moves, I would try them out on the hoop in the driveway. I read John McPhee's classic *A Sense of Where You Are*, and I can still remember tips I picked up from a *Sports Illustrated* article by Dave DeBusschere about how to draw fouls and play dirty without being detected. When I was old enough to venture across town on my own, I spent summer nights playing pickup games at a local park.

None of that came from my father. If it came from my family, it came from my older brother, Paul. He played basketball too, and whenever he had a pickup game at the house and there was a shortfall in numbers, I (four years younger but as tall as some of his friends) was plugged into the game. Scientifically, the verdict is still out about the effects of birth order on personality, but whatever future research shows (if anything), siblings do affect siblings. I learned to love basketball because my brother did.

I chose "love" quite deliberately. During my years of teenage obsession, basketball was more than a healthy pastime. It was a consuming dream because, like every American kid who learns to put a ball through a hoop, I wanted to end up in the NBA. That hopeless dream defined my life for several years. It determined how I spent my spare time, whom I spent it with, what books I read (not many!). My innermost dreams and desires were determined by what I brought up not from myself but from the players I watched and tried to mimic.

Hume's idea of "sympathy" is at work here too. "Reason is and ought only to be the salve of the passions, and can never pretend to any other office but to serve and obey them." Hume assumed that some passions were benevolent, particularly "sympathy," the capacity to "catch" and share the feelings, dispositions, moods, and thoughts of another. Sympathy is one of the main determinants of human character and behavior.

> No quality of human nature is more remarkable, both in itself and in its consequences, than the propensity we have to sympathize with others, and to receive by communication their inclinations and sentiments, however different from, or even contrary to our own. . . . To this principle we ought to ascribe the great uniformity we may observe in the humours and turn of thinking of those of the same nation; and 'tis much more probable, that this resemblance arises from sympathy, than from any influence of the soil and climate.[24]

We can be swept along by the emotions of others, so that their enthusiasms and loves become ours.

Jean-Jacques Rousseau likewise observed that desires are socially formed. Human beings possess a natural and altogether good form of self-regard or self-love. It is the self-love that leads us to eat when we're hungry, sleep when we're tired, have sex when we're horny. But in addition to this natural *amour de soi*, there is also the twisted form of self-love that we develop because of our involvement in human society, what Rousseau called *amour propre*. This sort of self-love is not healthy and good, but involves desire for goods that others possess. This sort of self-love is comparative and "purely negative." It doesn't "find satisfaction in our own well-being, but only in the misfortune of others."[25] For Rousseau, this insight exposed the tragic character of society: we cannot do without society, but society ruins us because it twists our healthy, natural self-love into a perverse shape.

These are the sorts of observations that led René Girard to formulate his notion of "mimetic desire." Desires are imitative. We want something because we see someone else wanting it. It is desirable not so much in itself but because we see someone else wanting it. Girard discerned this dynamic in Shakespeare's romantic comedies, where lovers sometimes fall in love because they have "borrowed" eyes from a rival. If another man loves Hermia, Hermia must be worth loving. Mimetic desire thus inevitably leads to rivalry, and rivalry, at least in all pagan *mythoi*, is resolved only by the mechanisms of scapegoating and sacrifice.

All of this to say that our desires and dreams, those qualities and ambitions that we think of as the most intimate things in our hearts and souls, those hopes that make us the unique people we are, are *not* ours alone. They are picked up from outside. It's "like father, like son" all over again. Our bodies are porous and permeable, and must be to survive. So too our souls, even to the innermost reaches of our identity, personality, character. Others and their dreams occupy the recesses of our hearts. Others dwell in us, even as we pitch our tent in them.

This changes the way we think of groups and societies. Psychologist Edwin Friedman observes that groups are like bodies in which each part affects all the other parts. The leader, Friedman says, is like the brain, but to get Friedman's point, we need to see that he doesn't think the brain is confined to the head. The brain diffuses into the entire body through the nervous system. I have memory in my hands when I play the piano, in my legs when I climb on a bicycle after many years of not riding. Brain activity flows through the whole body.

Just so, a leader's influence is not external to the organization the leader runs. The behavior of the leader affects the body. The leader spreads out in the organization, and the organization is in the leader. The key actions of leadership, Friedman thinks, are acts of self-definition, and "through his or her own self-definition, self-regulation, nonreactivity, and capacity to remain connected, a leader can make a critical difference. He or she can transmit a presence that has every bit as much capacity to regulate the various 'members' of the organism it is leading through the substances it is transmitting and through the way it responds to the substances it is receiving."[26] By distinguishing herself from the group, the leader comes to indwell the group as a whole. Groups operate that way because individual humans are permeable, porous, open to bring "inside" what is "outside."

All this means that "society" is primordial, basic to human experience. So are individuals. They are "equi-primordial." "Society" and "individuals" exist as distinct realities only by virtue of their interaction with each other, just as they can interact with each other only insofar as they are distinguishable. If the social environment around me didn't affect me, I wouldn't be who I am—an English-speaking, white American. If no one ever poured his or her passions into me, I would not be the unique individual that I am.

This is *not* the same as saying that society and individual are two opposing things that need to be kept in "balance." If we think of them as opposing things, external to one another, we're off on the wrong foot to begin with. Groups and individuals are irreducibly different, yet they are what they are only because each indwells the other. Individuals are individuals because society takes up residence in their soul, their thoughts, their habits, their table manners. But society is what it is only as a network of individuals. Individuals are dwelling places for others; society is a network of mutually indwelling components. Individuals exist only as they are indwelled by others; societies exist only as they are homes for individuals who make their homes in one another.

We have moved from thinking about the world around us that is always also in us to thinking about other people, who are also both around us and in us, just as we are around and in them. We've climbed up from objects to people, and we've found the same intricate pattern at work. We can't see everything clearly. But we can have some confidence that what we're seeing is starting to look like a trend.

What happens if we climb to another level and explore the most intimate relationships between human beings, relations not between casual acquaintances or even between family members but between lovers? What say we examine the pattern of romantic love and sex? If we discover the same shape yet again, we might begin to conclude that we are on to something, something big, as big as everything. We are finding clues. Something or someone seems to have left traces. When we get to the peak, we'll try to discover what's there and to see the whole landscape.

3

I Am His, He Is Mine

When trying to portray sex, some reach for the anatomy book. Traditionalists reach for poetry.

In Genesis, a man and woman become "one flesh." Robert Herrick imagined his "mortal part" as a vine crawling over and enthralling his "dainty Lucia," and earthy Robert Frost talked rurally of planting seeds. Donne found an image of sexual union in the combined blood of lover and beloved in a flea, while Andrew Marvell wanted to "roll all our strength and all / our sweetness up into one ball" so that he and his lover could "tear our pleasures with rough strife / through the iron gates of life." William Blake asked, "What is it men in women do require?" and "What is it women in men do require?" and gave the same answer to both: "The lineaments of Gratified Desire." Shakespeare's description is more vulgar, spoken by vulgar characters: united sexually, a man and woman form a new species, the "beast with two backs."[1]

It's a great mystery, and it's no accident that many religions and mystic philosophers draw on sexual imagery to describe human intimacy with God. The Swiss theologian Karl Barth observed that this sexual difference makes human beings most like God. There is an I-Thou within humanity that manifests the inner reciprocity, the differentiation and union, that is the life of the Trinity.[2] For millennia, Christians and Jews have allegorized the erotic Song of Songs, though few mystics were quite as explicit as Mechtild of Magdeburg: "Lord, now I am a naked soul / And you in yourself All-Glorious God. / Our mutual intercourse / Is eternal life without end."[3] Plato saw *eros* as the drive of the soul to return to its source, and the Indian mystic Kabir wrote, "My heart must cleave to my Lover / I must withdraw my veil, and / meet Him with all my body."[4] The longings of the mystic are like the longings of a woman to be united in one flesh with a man, the longings of a man to lose himself in the soft body and fluid embrace of a beloved woman.

A man enters a woman at her most private place, and there is one new thing in place of the two. Even before the man penetrates, the two have penetrated one another's space, if not one another's body. A man folds a woman in his arms, entangles his legs with hers, and the woman reciprocates. He nibbles at her breast. She kisses his neck. She touches and tastes while he breathes in her various natural and enhanced aromas.

This is a special form of human relation. In polite society, such close proximity is frowned upon.

Before a man penetrates, the two have probed each other's bodies with kisses. "May he kiss me with the kisses of his mouth," cries the woman at the beginning of the biblical Song of Songs. The mouth is the most intimate part of the face, the most intimate part of the body normally exposed in public. Eyes may be windows to the soul, but you can't see into me when I open my eyes. You might try to peer up my nostrils, or into my ear, but pretty quickly it gets too overcast to see much. When I open my mouth, though, there's a yawning chasm in the middle of my head, and without too much trouble you can see well into my interior, if you should wish to. Eyes are windows of the soul, but the mouth is the doorway to the body.

The mouth is the entry for food into our digestive tract, the gateway for bringing nourishment to the whole body. We drink water through the mouth, and we can breathe through the mouth. We eat, drink, and breathe the world into ourselves, the mouth being the main delivery system. So important and vulnerable a doorway needs guards, and the mouth is guarded by lips, backed up by teeth. The mouth is the most aggressive part of the face.

Doorways open each way. The mouth is a doorway in; it is also a doorway out. Saliva, mucous, vomit, and blood can escape through the mouth, but it is not only *physical* material that gets expelled through our mouths. Ideas, aspirations, compliments, songs, prayers, laments, screams and shrieks, and other expressions of our interior life move to the outside world through our mouths. Our words step past the curtain of the lips to present themselves to the waiting public.

For all their expressiveness, gesture and dance cannot express our desires or thoughts as articulately, as precisely, as the mouth. You can learn to write with the language you speak, and thus capture much of what can be spoken. But without voice, words lack the musical qualities of spoken language—timbre, pitch, volume, rhythm—and much of its emotional value.

And so the Bride of the Song of Songs wants a kiss, but not just any kiss. "May he kiss me with the kisses of his *mouth*." The Bride wants to be face-to-face and mouth to mouth with her Lover, to enter him and to open for his entry, to breathe into his mouth so that their breath becomes one breath.

A kiss is a synesthetic symphony. Lips touch lips, and with touch come taste and aroma. Not only is the kiss synesthetic: it is *mutual* synesthesia. The taste and the smell of two breaths mingle into one. Each touches the other as intimately as he or she is touched. It is, in Derrida's phrase, touching myself touching another (*se toucher toi*). A kiss is mutual consumption. A long, erotic kiss closely resembles eating, complete with bites and nibbles and licks. To kiss is to approach a one-flesh union, to become bone of bone, flesh of flesh, body of body.

A kiss, a touch of lip to lip or, more intimately, of tongue to tongue, is, next to sex itself, the most physically invasive custom we have. Holding hands, rubbing noses, hugging—these are intimacies, but they don't come close to the intimacy of the kisses of the mouth.

"One flesh" is no metaphor here. In a passionate kiss, the man enters the woman and the woman enters the man. They dwell in one another, breathe together with one breath. As kisses multiply and move from the mouth to the rest of the body, as a couple moves from kiss to intercourse, two bodies are bound so that it is no longer obvious where one ends and the other begins. A man indwells the woman even as the woman finds a home in the man's embrace.

We seem to be built for this.[5] The physical differences between men and women distinguish but at the same time encourage thoughts of union.[6] A man is physically built to enter a woman; a woman is physically capable of receiving him. There could hardly be a better fit if it were consciously designed. Perhaps it is.

Though one flesh in sexual union, the man and woman remain distinct. Each is irreducibly him- or herself. The man doesn't turn emotionally or physically into the woman, nor the woman into the man, nor do they form a third sex by their mingling. In their irreducible difference, though, they are united as one, as each opens to welcome the other and as each becomes a home for the other.[7]

Through intimate union of a woman and a man, the world gets peopled. Mutually indwelling sexual union is the most profoundly creative form of human contact. Businesspeople clasp hands when they sign a contract and create a new company. Hugs and kisses are exchanged all around at weddings and graduations, as people enter a new phase of life. Other sexual acts—autoerotic, homosexual, or one of the varieties of heterosexual sex—may be intense and intensely pleasurable personal experiences. But none of them is creative in the way heterosexual intercourse can be. None carries the potential to create a new human being. As Pope John Paul II frequently pointed out, heterosexual sex is both unitive and procreative.[8]

It seems that our inchoate suspicions at the end of chapter 2 have been confirmed. If human relationships in general display the form of mutual habitation, of interleaving and interweaving, we have some ground for believing that the most intimate of human relationships would manifest the same design even more intensely. And that's true. In sex, lovers give physical expression to a unity of mutual occupancy, as each enters into each. But that physical union signifies a relationship that is more than physical. In romantic relationships, lovers inhabit each other to such an extent that they become unfathomably "one flesh" and "one soul," sharing exultant joys and dismal sorrows as if they had one heart. In romantic love, two people live one life together.

"Birds do it, bees do it. Even educated fleas do it." It might seem that there's nothing distinctively human in human sexuality. All the poetry is a prudish effort to cover over our basic animality. Animals have all the equipment we have, and some are much better equipped. Male sea slugs discard their penises after sex and grow a new one. Some fish have barbs on their penises, and other fish have penises that grow out of their heads. Leatherback sea turtles are macho, with their four-foot penises, half their body length, beating the Argentine lake duck, whose penis looks like a corkscrew but can extend only a foot and a half. Most male birds don't have penises at all. Males fertilize by "kissing" the female's genitals with their own. Fish typically fertilize eggs outside the body. Marine flatworms are hermaphrodites, equipped with male and female organs, which saves a lot of muss and fuss and plenty of money wasted on romantic dinners. Male mammals, all male reptiles, and most other male land animals penetrate the vagina of the female to release semen and sperm that internally fertilize the female's egg. If lions wrote poetry, they could perhaps write about becoming "one flesh" with their lionesses.[9]

After mating with the queen bee, a drone's sexual organs explode, ending the life of the drone. A model of sexual efficiency, the queen collects semen from dozens of drones and stores it for later. New Mexico whiptale lizards are a matriarchalist's dream; all of them are female, and they need no fertilization from outside to reproduce. Human females gestate babies for nine months, but horses and camels are pregnant for over a year, and the sperm whale carries its young for nearly two years.

Granted, the equipment varies. But in the end, is human sex really any different from that? Birds do it, bees do it; even educated fleas do it.

But the birds and bees, even Ivy League fleas, don't care who's watching. Dogs copulate on the front lawn and masturbate against your leg when they feel the urge. The howls across the yard at night tell us that the old tomcat is back and that we should be expecting kittens in a couple of months.

Over the past half century we have gone some way to becoming tomcats and dogs. Everyone has seen the wild scenes from Woodstock, young men and women rolling in the mud, hairstyles obscuring sexual differences, maybe clothed, maybe not. Nude bodies and sex acts have become commonplace in the media. Porn sites are the most visited destinations on the web, and nighttime television is sexually explicit in ways that would make your grandmother cringe.

Still, we cannot quite escape shame. It's a rare thing to walk down the street of a major city and see people having sex. Public sex is still outlawed, and for most people the law isn't necessary.

We don't like our bodies exposed, and we don't want to have others looking on as we are intimate with another person. On-lookers—by definition, it would seem—make intimacy impossible. Even in a closed room, in the dark, under the sheets, some feel exposed and want to run and hide.[10] Shame is a negative experience and emotion, but it makes a positive point about human beings: we are not cats and dogs, and our sexual habits are not merely physical and biological.

Moderns think of sexual desire as relief of physical need or the pursuit of pleasure. Post-Freud, sex has become a form of hydraulics, a matter of pressure and release. Not too long ago, the vulgar phrase "exchange of fluids" was in currency in warnings about the dangers of "unprotected" sex. But if sexual acts are merely physical processes, merely a matter of inserting this protrusion into this hole, merely a matter of joining body parts and fluids—if that's all it is, why the shame? Why the veils? Why the poetry?

Becoming one flesh, the sexual dwelling-in of a man and woman, is too mysterious to be done out in the open. The anatomists and clinicians are wrong, and the poets right. For whatever reason, humans reach for veils, including the veil of poetry. That suggests that the physical exchange, the physical indwelling, signifies something beyond the slap and thump and rub of two closely proximate bodies in motion.

Maybe the truth is aesthetic: sexual attraction exhibits human delight in beauty. That is often part of sexual attraction, but certainly not the whole of it. Sometimes beauty is not the issue at all. Perverse forms of human sexuality—sadism, masochism, domination—are not about beauty, but have to do with the strange pleasure of transgression or power. In our racist past, and still in the present, black human bodies were considered at once repulsive and irresistibly attractive. Besides, our films and photo spreads deceive us, with their elegant bodies and athletic sex. Sex between real people is not like that. Most of us have

41

bodies far less sleek-smooth than the ones we see in the movies, and our sex is far clumsier than the balletic eroticism around us. It's often more comic than erotic.

I submit that the physical form of sex points quite directly to the thing it signifies. Sex involves the union of two into one, and this union is a union of mutual envelopment and mutual indwelling. Precisely *that* is the physical sign of what human sexuality aims at. It's not a yellow intersection sign posted a mile away from the actual intersection. It's more like the Christian sacraments, a sign that participates in the reality it signifies, a sign that in its very physical form reveals the outline of the reality it signifies. The physical indwelling points to a personal entanglement and intertwining that persist beyond the bedroom.

The romantic paradigm of modern love is so well known as to be trite: strangers meet, "fall in love," and decide to spend the rest of their lives together. In many cases, the worlds they inhabited before meeting did not overlap at all. My parents knew my wife's parents for years before the two of us met, but we had never met until we were three years into college. None of my four married children knew their spouses before young adulthood. Most come to marriage with a life story, an ongoing conversation about the world that does not include the other.[11]

Falling in love means revising that life story and ongoing conversation so that it includes the new loved one. The man starts telling his story in a way that includes his first sight of his wife, their friendship and romance, the proposal scene, the wedding. Wives do the same, only better, because they recall all the details guys forget. Each begins to indwell the narrative of the other.

This can't be a single addition to a story that remains unchanged in other respects. Because the man and woman end up married, their first encounter and conversation become fraught with possibility. On that enchanted evening, he saw a stranger and heard her laughter across a crowded room. He had seen beautiful strangers before, and heard them laughing across crowded rooms. Nothing is more common. Yet this becomes a critical moment in the story because of what happens after. The whole story changes because *one* new character is added. What used to be a straightforward melody line becomes a fugue, line intertwined with line. What used to be a simple melody line gets harmonized; it turns polyphonic. His life dwells in hers, and hers in his. He is hers, and she is his.

In a number of his books, the late philosopher Robert Solomon described the dynamics of romantic love as a process of redefining the self. We have a particular identity, but when we meet that special person, we redefine who we are. Our hopes and dreams now encompass a partner and are encompassed by his or her dreams and hopes. Solomon thinks that this accounts for the confusion and disorientation, the palpitations and nausea that accompany the process we call "falling in love." What scares us is not only the reality and near presence of another. What scares a couple is that each is becoming a new person.[12] Each person's life expands at least enough to include the other's. Each is present to the other "in nearly all the horizons of everyday conduct."[13] This happens over time, in ongoing conversation, as the two lovers combine and integrate the separate conversations of which they had previously been a part into a single, unified conversation. It takes time, a lifetime, for one life to fully indwell another.

Sexual love is a desire to dwell in a person not only physically but emotionally and personally as well. It is a desire for the mutual indwelling of sexual union to become a figure of a life lived together as one complex entity, one story line, with a hero now joining the heroine.[14]

It's not just the two lovers that get redefined and reperceived. Because they are each entangled with others and with the world, when each is transformed by a unique mutuality with a lover, their world changes. The beloved gives new color to everything. The beach where they spent their honeymoon, the restaurant where he proposed, the moment of their first kiss or their first night in bed, every place they go together is sanctified by association with their love, and in their imaginations, each place is tinged by the beloved. The world is experienced afresh in the light of their mutual love.

Robert Alter has noticed two sorts of romantic or erotic poetry. In much of the world's erotic literature, "the body in the act of love often seems to displace the rest of the world." The lover sweeps his beloved off her feet and out of her place, whisking her to a private world just for the two of them. The world is lost to lovers. In some romantic poetry—Alter is writing about the Song of Songs—"the world is constantly embraced in the very process of imagining the body. The natural landscape, the cycle of the seasons, the beauty of the animal and floral realm, the profusion of goods afforded through trade, the inventive skill of the artisan, the grandeur of cities, are all joyfully affirmed as love is affirmed."[15] Solomon is no courtly lover who abandons the world and all to chase after his bride. When he turns from the world to dwell in his beloved, he rediscovers his world *in* her.

That sounds slurpily poetic, but it is as practical as can be. Sociologists Peter Berger and Hansfried Kellner note that a man's relationships with his male friends "rarely survive the marriage, or, if they do, are drastically redefined by it." This is not (necessarily) the result of any malicious sabotage by the wife. Instead, "the husband's image of his friend is transformed as he keeps talking about his friend with his wife." Even if the two don't talk about prior friendships, the "mere presence of the wife forces him to see his friend differently." Whether the wife likes or dislikes the friend, the husband's image of his friend changes. The conversation that takes place within the marriage so dominates the world of the two married partners that all the world is remolded in it. Everyone and everything the couple encounters are talked through, and by those conversations everything and everyone become part of the mutual story weaved by the lovers. As the lovers indwell one another's lives, so they envelop the world into their mutual story. The world that surrounds them is brought into the conversation that makes up their identity as a couple.[16]

The substantial reality of the entanglement of lovers is most clearly evident when they are pried from each other at death. For a year and more after my mother died, my father would look up from his paper to tell her some interesting tidbit he knew she would enjoy. When my wife's uncle died, his widow said that she felt as if she had lost half of herself. She wasn't exaggerating. Her husband had lived in her so long that pulling him out was like having a heart transplant.

Romantic drama often turns on the inability of a man to reshape his world and network of relationships around his relationship with his beloved. In Shakespeare's *Much Ado about Nothing*, Claudio's superficial attraction to Hero is shattered when he thinks that she has been unfaithful. The villian, Don John, convinces him that Hero is a strumpet, and Claudio viciously rejects her during her wedding ceremony. The drama of the scene obscures its unreality. Any sane Claudio would talk to his Hero to get her side of the story. Claudio never does. Unrealistic as it is, Claudio's eagerness to reject Hero is thematically appropriate. Despite his protestations of love for Hero, he has not become a new man. She does not dwell in his life powerfully enough to redefine his relationships with his male friends. His male friends, the boy's club of the military company, still dominate his perceptions. His world hasn't been rearranged in conversation with Hero. His world has not become Hero-colored.

After the wedding where Claudio summarily tosses Hero aside, Beatrice and Benedick finally profess their love for one another. Like the lovers he has always scorned, Benedick professes that he is willing to do anything for Beatrice. When she says, "Kill Claudio," Benedick comically backpedals: "Not for the wide world. We'll be friends first." But Beatrice will not settle for anything but a complete overhaul of Benedick's loyalties. She refuses to settle in the suburbs of his good pleasure. If she is not the most important thing in the world to him, if he does not find his whole world in her and see it through her, then she wants none of his passionate professions of love.

The mutual indwelling of lovers is a kind of mutual possession. Each has ownership of the other, because each has become so much a part of the other that the two can barely be distinguished. Mutual possession can go badly wrong. Possession can become domination. The desire for assimilation can turn cannibalistic, so that the other gets absorbed and ceases to be other. Mutual indwelling by which two become one can be perverted into an erasure of difference.

Christos Yannaras has movingly described the tragic tendencies in our hopeless thirst for relation: "Lacking the knowledge of how to exist in the *mode* of relation," our desire is "constantly disappointed." We don't know how to share, don't know how to give ourselves. We are self-protective. We don't want to lose ourselves in the other, so we cannibalize the other and digest the other into us. The tragic potential of love is this: "If the taste of fullness is a communion of life with the Other, our natural drive destroys this communion, turning it into a possessive and demanding domination of the Other."[17] Our demands, our "voracity" and "need," are all forms of resistance to the life-giving communion we long for: "The instinct for self-preservation, the drive to possess, the thirst for self-assertion" all "alienate the relation, set limits to coexistence, destroy participation." All "fight against love."[18]

To love truly, one must not only move ecstatically out from himself to dwell in another, must not only open up a home in himself for the beloved, but must do so in a way that preserves the irreducible *otherness* of the beloved. Lovers penetrate one another only when they do not eradicate the individuality that makes their love possible. Love must *in*gest without *di*gesting the other. Love *only* exists as a union of mutual indwelling, signified by the kiss that is the kiss of the mouth, by the folding of each into the other that is signified in sexual communion.

We've climbed high enough on this path to see quite a bit of the landscape. It's not all the same. It's richly varied and tangled as a jungle. But if we stare long enough from our current vantage point, the whirl and twirl begin to make sense. We begin to see a recurring configuration and a repetitive contour. The world is coming into focus in all its knotted glory.

Many have believed sex is very close to the peak of the mountain. In some religions, sex provides the key insight into the nature of things, offering a vista extending to the edge of the horizon. Sex is a trace of the divine within the human world. The world is full of throbbing, teeming energy, and in some religions sex provides a way to participate in that energy. Sex is often a symbol for the religious desire to unite with whatever is beyond all nature. The goddess coyly calls from behind the veil, enticing the worshiper to act the part of a lover by lifting the veil and drawing near. In Vajrayana Buddhism, a disciple who has recognized the void engages in tantric sexual practices to attain the final stages of bliss and enlightenment. Christians believe that the advent of Jesus the Bridegroom is the center of all human history, and the last book of the Bible indicates that the human story will be consummated by the great wedding feast of the Lamb.

We can formulate a syllogism of sorts: if sex is a clue to the cosmos and its history, and if sex involves the mutual penetration and habitation of lovers, then we may conclude that the shape of the world resembles the shape of human love. We suspect that time itself might have an "erotic" shape. It is the business of chapter 4 to stoke up those very suspicions.

4

Presence of the Past

Since I started this paragraph, I've written and deleted sentence fragments that I'll soon forget and no one else will ever see. I've looked out the window to see who is passing on the sidewalk, and I've been startled by the sounds of library rearrangement across the room. In a few minutes, I'll check my email again, though there's no good reason to do so. And that's not even to bring up the fact that during the past few moments my heart has been beating regularly, my digestive system has been at work, and a few hundred or a few thousand skin cells have flaked off and joined the rest of the dust in the air and on the desk.

Events happen constantly. Time ticks relentlessly on.

Time was one of the central puzzles for ancient thinkers because time posed the problem of change. Early on, some Greeks thought that change was the most fundamental reality of all. "Heraclitean flux" is a cliché of pop philosophy. Time waits for no one, and time means change. You can't step in any river twice. Nothing is ever the same moment by moment.

But there were Greeks who wanted to say, "Hold on, now. Sure, change happens, but not all of those changes change *you*. You are the same you whether you are looking out the window or distracted by library noise. There's an unchanging you that does and suffers all those things that change. If there were no unchanging you, there'd be no way to know things were changing in the first place."

Whatever it is, this unchanging me can't be the physical, bodily me. Over time my body has changed quite a lot. I used to have hair and no beard, but now . . . you can guess. I used to be able to see at a distance, but now . . . I used to weigh . . . never mind.

What's true of *me* is true of everything else too. Leaves have fallen onto the sidewalk outside, and they've accumulated in the cracks between blocks. The edges of the sidewalk have chipped. The wooden bench used to be in better shape than it is, and the locust tree outside used to be much smaller. Turn back the clock twenty-five years, and all of that would be different.

Yet, the anti-Heracliteans will insist, those things remain the things they are through all sorts of changes. Some changes will be so massive that the thing becomes something else. The tree might burn down, or be cut into boards for lumber. At that point, it would become ash or lumber or a tree house, no longer a tree. Before it gets there, though, it can undergo all sorts of changes and remain the same thing. I've never been in a disfiguring accident, and I've never lost a limb. But I'm confident that if I had done so I would remain who I am. I would be an armless me or a me with a bright scar from the chemical accident, but I'd still be me.[1]

Since the bodily me isn't the unchanging me, the unchanging me has to be something immaterial, a soul or some other ghostly presence high above or deep down things.

It's this sort of problem that pressed philosophers to invent concepts like the Platonic ideas or the Aristotelian ideas of substance. For Platonists, ideas are the eternal, unchangeable forms in which all material things participate. Because they participate in an eternal idea, things have a persistent identity through time. Because they aren't identical to those ideas, they don't stay the same. *Real* things don't change. Whatever changes shows by that very change that it is not entirely real. If it were real, it would be fully *real*ized, and wouldn't need to change. Only the ideas are fully real.

Aristotle wasn't satisfied with that. He claimed that the form of a thing contains a dynamic quality that drives it toward its fulfillment. A seed contains the potential to become a tree. As the seed grows to reach its potential, it looks, smells, feels, tastes different. At the same time, something has to stay the same through the process of change. Changes have to happen *to* something, and if that something isn't somehow the same, then change can't really happen. If there's not a stable me as my hair falls out, then the event of falling hair is not happening to me; the hairy me simply disappears and a bald me comes to be. That's not change. It's replacement.

For Aristotle, change occurs as a subject—the thing or person that undergoes change—loses a "privation," as it loses something it lacks. A man lacks the ability to write; he learns to write, and by losing the privation of the ability to write, he becomes a man-who-is-capable-of-writing. A new positive quality—"ability to write"—now describes the man, joining other qualifiers like "with black hair" and "5 feet 10 inches tall" and "native Greek speaker." A block of marble lacks shape, but as the sculptor shapes it, it loses that lack, and takes on a new form—the form of a man or a griffin or a Corinthian capital.

Change can go in the opposite direction too, if somebody with a large hammer beats the marble statue to smithereens, or the man who knows how to write comes down with a debilitating dementia that deprives him of that skill. In that case, the form's "ability to write" and "having the shape of a man" no longer qualify the man and the stone.

Overlaying this notion of change is Aristotle's distinction of substance and accidents. A man is already a substance, and when he takes on the form of "being able to write" he takes on an "accidental" property. The man is unchanged; the change is on the surface of his substance. Some changes are substantial, changes that bring a different thing into being. That's what happens to the marble block as it is shaped into a statue. The marble block had matter but no sculpted shape, and the sculptor gives it shape. It becomes a new thing, a new substance—a sculpture of a man. When an acorn becomes an oak, a substantial change takes place, since the acorn moves from being an unformed or potential tree to an actual tree.

These are honorable philosophical attempts to make sense both of the reality of change and of the persistence of identity through change. They are valiant efforts to make philosophical sense of our temporality. Yet they all share a fundamental flaw, which is the tendency to treat time as if it were external to things. For Plato, the thing *is* the form in which it participates, but that means the thing is essentially timeless. That's a problem, because if there's one thing that is obvious about the world, about you and me, it is that time happens, time exists, and that we aren't timeless.

Aristotle tries to build change into his system, but he doesn't wholly succeed. Aristotle says that substances are basic sorts of things. Humans and horses, tigers and trees are primary substances. Yet these primary substances are composed of form and matter, and so are made of components that are more basic than substances. Substances aren't basic after all. But if Aristotle's original idea of change is correct, then there has to be a subject that remains the same through the change. What *is* it that stays the same when an acorn changes to a tree, or a block of marble to a statue? It can't be the acorn or the block. It can't be the form either, since the statue has a different form from the unsculpted block of wood. It's hard to see how it could be the matter, since the tree obviously contains more matter than the acorn, and the statue contains less marble than the block. Yet change must happen *to* something. What that something *is* Aristotle never quite clarifies.

According to the American theologian Robert Jenson, the fundamental problem of both Greek religion and Greek philosophy was the problem of time, and the fundamental agenda was to escape time. Greek religion asks, "Can it be that all things pass?" Hesiod told of Chronos devouring his children, but then he added a hopeful story about the overthrow of Chronos by Zeus, who establishes justice, order, fixity. "Their religion was the determination that 'Time' not be supreme, that he be overthrown by a true 'Father of gods and men.' Greek religion was a quest for a rock of ages, resistant to the flow of time, a place or part or aspect of reality immune to change."[2]

Greek philosophy is an effort to discover what stays the same. In Jenson's reading, Aristotle assured Athens that "Being as such neither comes to be nor perishes." According to Aristotle, "The Unbounded has no beginning . . . but seems rather to be the Beginning of all other realities, and to envelope and control them. . . . This is the Divine." Sometimes this divine reality was called Zeus, and he was defined as the "true religious object," the object of worship, veneration, devotion: "timelessness as such."[3]

But we never encounter timelessness. Everything around us passes away. So, "if there is the divine, it must . . . be above or behind or beneath or within the experienced world. It must be the bed of time's river, the foundation of the world's otherwise unstable structure, the track of heaven's hastening lights." All Greek religion and philosophy was a metaphysical "quest for the timeless ground of temporal being." Greek religion and philosophy are quests, searches; because the timeless ground is not immediately available, it must be pursued. We apprehend God "by penetrating through the temporal experienced world to its atemporal ground."[4]

As a result, "theology is . . . essentially negative." All we can say is what God is *not* because everything we know in this world is temporal and God is timeless. The central religious insight, which spilled over into philosophy, was about God's distance from us: "We are in time and God [or the Form of the Good, or substance] is not, and just so our situation is desperate."[5]

Escape from time is one aspect of the modern effort to isolate the inner me from the outer world. Moderns don't seek timelessness in a Platonic world of ideas or among the deathless gods. They seek timelessness within, in a thinking thing that stands apart from the world of time and change. The whole point of Descartes's retreat within was to find a safe place where knowledge was fixed, certain, undeniable. The back door of doubt that Descartes tried was also a back door to changeless, pure certainty.

As we've seen, that doesn't work. We are distinct from the world, but we are simultaneously in a relation of mutual habitation with the world. We are temporal beings in a mutable world. We change, and the world changes around us. As the world changes, it changes us; as we change, we change the world. That's the way things are.

Time isn't a problem to be solved. It's the wonder and mystery of human existence. Without change in the world, we couldn't change either. Without change, we wouldn't exist at all. Unless our lungs process the air we receive, moving oxygen from the atmosphere into the cells that make up our bodies, we can't stay alive. Water and food undergo change in our digestive system, or we can't get the nutrients we need from them. I'd still be a few inches long, if I had survived at all, if the world hadn't entered me, changed into me, so that I could change. And the changes we undergo are more than biological. If we couldn't change personally and morally, we'd be locked into our current illusions, addictions, habits, dead ends, ignorance. No course correction would be possible. Change is the possibility of redemption.

So let us say that we've reconciled ourselves to time. Suppose we say that time is of the *essence* of things, and that change is good, very good. Let us say that we are temporal beings, and that our temporality goes "all the way down." There's no hidden timelessness deep within or high above in a world of ideas. Our souls as well as our bodies, our selves as well as our physical forms, experience time and all that goes with it, change and growth and degeneration and novelty and obsolescence. Let us say all that, but then we are still faced with a series of puzzles. Here it is not the Greeks but Augustine who is the main spokesperson.[6]

Augustine says that he knows what time is until someone asks. He knows the experience of passing time. He knows early, long, and late. He knows that he can think about segments of time as if they were segments of lines, as though time could be parceled out into sections. But once he tries to stare time down, *really* stare it down face-to-face, he is struck dumb. Time isn't really a line, because lines exist in space, and time isn't a kind of space. How then can we measure it?

One of the puzzles is the basic sectioning of time into past, present, and future. The past clearly does not exist. I am no longer a thirteen-year-old boy obsessed with basketball. I was, but am not. That time of my life doesn't exist. Once, a great iron curtain was stretched across Europe, running straight through Berlin, but not so long ago that curtain fell. Once George Bush was president of the United States. All of these past events and experiences happened, but they don't keep happening. They are once-for-all, like every event. Their effects continue, but the events don't. The time when they happened doesn't exist now.

For equally obvious reasons, the future doesn't exist either because it hasn't happened yet. President Obama's successor is unknown at present, and hasn't assumed office. The outcome of the latest war in Iraq is uncertain. My next grandchild has not yet been born, though I am confident that there is at least one more to come.

If the past and future don't exist, at least we have the present, but Augustine is as bewildered by the present as he is by the past and the future. At this exact second, the next second is future. That future second doesn't exist yet, but as soon as I said "this exact second"—in fact, before I finish the phrase—that exact second doesn't exist anymore either. So the present doesn't seem to exist anymore than any other time. It's over before we can say "over." The future doesn't exist because it hasn't happened; the past doesn't exist because it has; the present exists, but only for a split second before it joins with all the nonexistent past moments.

Still, Augustine says, we can measure time. When we speak, we can recognize "long" and "short" syllables, even though the "lengths" are of time and not of space. Augustine doesn't think we measure the sounds themselves, but rather the psychic impression of sounds, and that is because we can "measure" the length of words, or of music, even when the sounds have gone silent. How can we measure syllables that are not being spoken, unless those time segments exist somehow in the soul? Besides, we can measure out periods of silence, pauses between syllables and words. We must again be measuring things in the soul. Time overlaps, the past held in memory and the future held in anticipation. We can apprehend time only by retaining what has been and anticipating what will be.

All of this together leads Augustine to define time as a "distension" or stretching-out of the soul. We anticipate, and so we experience the reality of future; we hope for what is not yet. We remember, and so we experience the reality of the past; we recall what has been. And we do this in the evanescent present that passes like mist before the sun. Our soul is stretched out toward the past and future, strung up on the ever-changing present between the poles of memory and desire. Augustine doesn't intend to reduce time to psychology. We live in time, and movement and time correlate to one another. Time has an objective dimension, but "lived time is made determinate and explicable by time measured by psychic distension."[7] Because of this, he says that the past and future exist as aspects of the present moment. Past and future are the past-of-the-present and the future-of-the-present. Past and future are not realities in the world.

This is not an entirely bad answer to the questions Augustine poses, but he shares too much of the ancient disquiet with time. It still smacks too much of an effort to hide from time.

Eugen Rosenstock-Huessy argued that time isn't just a succession of present moments nor simply a distension in the soul. More than Augustine, he emphasizes the objective, real character of time and the human involvement in the world that gives time its shape.

Time is not a container with hard edges that stay the same no matter what is happening within. It is not like a metal cistern where some people murder while others make love. We get fooled into thinking of time like this because we are seduced into thinking that time is the ticks of a clock, those regular monotonous moments that never speed up or slow, never change no matter what is going on, those ticks that can keep track of anything and everything. Mechanical timepieces are among the great innovations of modern society, and we can't do without them. We wouldn't know when to show up for the train, or when the train is likely to show up, unless schedules get coordinated, and the clock is the most efficient way we've found to coordinate them. So, then, several hearty cheers for mechanical timepieces. Still, the time they keep is not time in its fullness.

Time is molded by what takes place within it. It slows down to a crawl, sometimes because we are experiencing something traumatic, sometimes because we are experiencing something indescribably wonderful. Several times in my life, the world has drifted into slow motion while I was in the middle of a sports game, or reading an absorbing book, or writing a book.[8]

Rosenstock-Huessy doesn't think these shapes and molds of time are merely subjective. The ref throws up the ball and a clock begins, and we are in the "time of the game." There's a clock going, but the time of the game is not identical to the time that elapses on the game clock. In baseball, there is no clock, but there is the "time of the game," a segment of time that is determined by the thing that is taking place within it.

Ever the teacher, Rosenstock-Huessy thought that the classroom was a particularly good illustration of the way time is molded into a "body of time." Each teaching situation is a union of past and future, of old and new. The teacher is the "old" one, usually in years but always in exposure to and study of the material. A young pastor who preaches to a congregation much older in years is still expected to be "older" in the texts preached. The student is always the "youth," who comes to the time of teaching with the aspiration to grow up to become like the teacher. This union of past and future, old and young, forms a present time. In terms of clock time, the present time of the class or sermon or game might be of varying lengths, but whatever its length in clock terms, the time of the class is a segment of time with a quality, shape, and limits of its own.

On a larger scale, history is divided into periods. Events and epochs begin and end, and their beginnings and endings don't always correspond to the calendar. The Victorian era really was a distinct period of history, not merely because Queen Victoria ruled but also because England during that era had a more or less unified national culture, international program, political aspirations. World War I shattered the naive optimism of the Victorians and opened a new era of history. Luther's protests against the Catholic Church were not unique. Reformers before Luther had attacked papal abuses, and some even anticipated certain of Luther's theological distinctives. But when Luther challenged the church, many factors converged to create a new era. The Reformation was a highly complex series of events, but it marked and created a new stage of European history, as did the French and Russian Revolutions.

Rosenstock-Huessy's observations on time's malleability take us back toward the themes of this book. Time isn't external to the events that happen in it. Time and incident together define a time-body, because the event envelops and penetrates the time even as the time envelops and penetrates the event. Instead of saying that the past and future don't exist, or saying that they exist only as dimensions of the present, Rosenstock-Huessy says that the past and future meet and mix to form a present. And that insight helps us grasp not only the quality of a "body of time" like a class time or a game time but also the nature of time itself. It helps us to see that time, like the other features of the world that we have examined in this book, is structured by mutually indwelling, by the habitation of distinct times in one another.

We've come full circle—though it's too twisted to be a circle. When we inquired into my relation to the world, we discovered that I exist, I am, only if the world comes into me as I come into the world. When we asked about the relationships between human beings, we found that human beings are snarled together in a variety of ways and through a variety of media: we impress ourselves on the soft plastic of others more than we can know. When we examined human sexuality, we found that intense human relationships, relationships between lovers, are physically and spiritually entangled relationships of mutual habitation. Our ponderings and musings on time have come to the same conclusion. We keep seeing traces of the same curious profile as we pass by these features of our world, and it's becoming a familiar one. We hope to see it more clearly, because we're beginning to wonder, Whose profile, if anyone's, might it be?

Augustine was right: memory is one mode of the past's presence in the present. The past is present *within* me. Memory is not, however, the only mode of the past's presence. I am sitting on a chair that was here before I came into the library this morning. The chair was made by someone or some machine a long time before it arrived in this library for me to sit in. It's a product from the past inhabiting the present. I'm sitting in a building that was erected in its first form in the late nineteenth century. It's one of the oldest buildings in town, but every building within view was built before I was born. At the local diner a couple of doors down, you can find pictures of the city when it was first established, and you can see some of the buildings. In the pictures, the buildings are on the edges of a dusty dirt road, horses being the main mode of transportation. Today, even in a small town in northern Idaho, there is a paved road running straight through town with traffic lights and *everything*. That happened before I got here too, the roads probably paved before I was born, which was an awfully long time ago.

My body bears traces of the past too. There is a scar where the surgeon made an incision to repair a torn Achilles tendon. There's the empty space at the back of my mouth where the dentist removed a dead tooth, a cap on one of my front teeth that's been there since I broke the tooth falling off a horse when I was a boy, and there are gaps further back in my mouth, should you care to explore it, where I used to have impacted wisdom teeth. On my left hand is a ring that's been there for over thirty years now, and when I take it off there's an indentation circling my finger. My body is a placard of the past, a living past that invades the present.

The past isn't the present. Augustine was right about that too. But the past that is different from the present inhabits the present. I inhabit a world that is shaped the way it is because of the past. So do you. So do all of us who have not lived through an atomic explosion or a tsunami that wipes out the accumulated bric-a-brac of the past. The past isn't *the* present, but it *is* present.

The past is present, and so is the future, though in a different fashion. The future buildings of Moscow, Idaho, are not
visible on the street, nor are the scars of future surgeries (or
floggings) visible on my body. But the future inhabits the present in massive ways nonetheless. I'm writing this chapter now,
on May 29, 2013. That is the present day. But I'm writing this
book now because I know that come early December, I'm supposed to send this book manuscript off to the publisher. That
future event determines my present activities, all the more so
because I affixed my signature to a contract some time in the
past and obligated myself—in ways that I will regret sometime
in November[9]—to finish the book manuscript by that particular
deadline. Futures are always determining the present in these
ways. I rarely do anything during a day that isn't oriented to
some future, a hoped-for completion that has not yet arrived.

And my present is also determined by the futures of past
people. The builders of the building I'm sitting in built in anticipation of a future completion. Their future is now past to me,
but without their future aspirations to complete the building,
there would be no building, and my past and present would be
quite different. I'd be sitting in an empty lot, for starters, if I
was sitting in the same location at all. Not only my future but
also the futures of past humans inhabit my present. You might
call this interpenetration of times "subjective," but that's not
an accurate picture of what is going on. The future time for
completion is set—in the case of the book, with a legally binding contract. And that future time for completion is affecting
not only my state of mind (which is presently calm, but will
grow toward anxiety as the deadline approaches) but also my
activities. My location on the present day (at the library), my
activities during a few afternoon hours (banging away elegantly
on my old MacBook), my posture, my coffee consumption, my
reaction to the people around me—all these objective factors
about my present are determined and shaped by the future.

We can in fact make the point more strongly: there can be *no present* unless past and future inhabit it. Or, to say the same thing, there is no time without the mutual indwelling of distinct times. Augustine was right to stress that without memory we can have no experience of time at all. Leonard, the hero of Christopher Nolan's film *Memento*, suffers from severe short-term memory loss. He can't remember from one day to the next whom he met or how he got where he is. His life is a series of presents, and those moments don't constitute an experience of time. He has no sense of change because he has no recollection that things were different yesterday.[10] Unless the past remains, at least in memory, we can't know how long we've been talking, or waiting for the bus, or walking the Manhattan sidewalk.

Without the past in the present, each day would be a blank slate. The past has to be present not only in memory but also in the form of artifacts. If it's not, I have to remake myself, and my world, fresh each morning, each moment. I just went to the microwave to heat my coffee. When I touch the cup, it's still hot. The past event of heating the coffee inhabits the present, and I wouldn't experience this present without that past event. Without the habitation of the past in the present, there is no present, no present as we actually know and experience it. Similarly, without the future indwelling my present, I'm stymied. I have nothing to do because I have nowhere to go, nowhere I even *want* to go. Past, present, and future are irreducibly different. But they exist as the distinctive times that they are only because of their relation with other times, because each inhabits the other.

Time, in short, manifests the same spiral, twirling, and curving pattern as my relation to the world, as my personal identity, as sexuality, as the relation of the individual to the social world. In every case, we confront a pattern of mutual habitation, mutual indwelling. And in every case, this pattern is *necessary* for grasping the reality of the world as it is. As we climb higher and take a breath, I hope we might be on to something. Don't you?

5

Word in Word in World

How can marks on paper, or pixels on a computer screen, or vibrations of the air transfer the thoughts of one person to another? Maybe that's the wrong question. Is transferring thoughts what those marks and pixels and vibrations are for?

Many have thought so. First an idea pops into your mind; then that thought gets translated into marks or sounds; then those marks and sounds carry your thoughts to another person. When she sees those marks or hears those sounds, the same thoughts that *you* started with pop into her mind. Words carry a nano-packet of information that gets moved from my head to yours along the way of sight or sound.

Not everyone has thought that visual marks and sounds are equally effective in accomplishing this task. For Plato and Aristotle, a spoken word is a sign of the first order, a direct sonic expression of a thought. A spoken word has a direct connection with the speaker, since it depends (for Aristotle, who lived before recording devices) on the immediate presence of the person. A *written* word, though, is a sign of a sign, a visual mark of a spoken word, which is itself a sign of the real deal—namely, the thought in my head. Written signs are a second step removed from the ideas of the speaker, and so less reliable. Thoughts translate pretty well into sound. Thoughts don't come through as clearly in the mode of visual signs.

In a practical sense, this is understandable. If I'm talking to you and it becomes clear that you misunderstand, I can restate my point. If you're reading this book and you misunderstand, there's little I can do. My written words go off on their own, wandering errantly through the world, a prodigal son sent into a far country.[1] Theoretically, this makes less sense. Plato and Aristotle are suspicious of visual marks on paper for the same reason they are suspicious of material things in general. Sounds seem more spiritual, but marks on paper are unavoidably physical.[2]

On these premises, written language presents a great mystery. If I were trained in classical Greek, I could read the words Plato and Aristotle actually wrote. But it's not easy to understand them. Even the best-trained classicist isn't sure what all the words mean and can't catch all the connotations they might have carried in classical Athens. But the texts aren't utterly opaque. We can speak with confidence about the "thought" of Plato or Aristotle. We know that Homer wrote about Hector's death and Achilles's triumph. We know that Odysseus got home to slaughter the suitors and lead Penelope to his olive-tree bed. We know that Plato had a doctrine of ideas, that he was suspicious of poets, and that he believed in the justice of the soul and of the republic. We know of Aristotle's broad curiosity. We know that Aeneas escaped the flames of Troy and founded Rome, and we know of the probing questions of Augustine.

It's as if we had a way of wiretapping the brains of long-dead philosophers. But we don't: ancient Athens is one place we can be fairly certain that the National Security Agency had no listening devices. All we have are their books. It's not perfect, but it's what we have and it's nearly as good as a wiretap. An entire family of academic disciplines—classics—and thousands of books and essays in many languages, even a fair number of movies, derive from ancient Greek and Latin works. They are all of them based on the premise that we have some fair idea of what the heck they meant.

The *only* thing that enables us to do this is language. Which is to say, marks on ancient paper.[3]

Still, I have serious doubts that "communicating thought" is the best way to describe the purpose of language. Language communicates thoughts, of course, but that's not the only thing language does, and probably not the main one. Intellectuals and academics and philosophers think this is what language is for because it's what *they* use language for. But when the baseball slips sideways out of my hand and begins sailing toward an unsuspecting bystander, my cry of "Duck!" or "Watch out!" isn't an attempt to communicate thoughts from my brain to the bystander's. It's an effort to prevent an accident, and to save myself the trouble of a lawsuit. I don't think much before shouting, and I don't want the bystander to think either. I want her to "Duck!" and "Watch out!"

Imperatives and warnings have a pragmatic aim. When the commander says "Fire!" the soldier fires. He may well spend the rest of his life thinking about what he did, but in the moment he doesn't think—at least, he shouldn't. He *fires*. The commander has taught his troops in the past, but by the time he yells "fire" the teaching is over. He gives the order to get the troops to *do* something, not to *think* something; he's not *teaching* them, he's *moving* them, and he uses language to do it. Mark Antony wants to move people too. When he addresses the Roman crowds at Caesar's funeral, he communicates ideas, but his main goal is to arouse the mob's indignant passions. If I'm writing copy for an ad agency, I want to arouse desires, and I hope potential customers *don't* think much about their purchases.

And then there are those peculiar uses of language that bring new states of affairs into existence. These "performative utterances" like "I now pronounce you man and wife" aren't communicating ideas. We can utter our ideas with words. We can make other people do things with our words. We can also *do* things with words.[4]

Maybe we should say this: While language has many different uses, the most *basic* and important is the indicative statement of facts or ideas. That's where we start. Other forms of language are "deviations" or, more neutrally, "derivations" from that baseline use.

Popular as that view is, it doesn't fit the facts either. In actual life, we don't start out hearing or speaking indicatives. Toddlers first hear commands—"Don't touch that candle!"—and warnings—"Keep away from the steps!"[5] But when children first use language, they use words as labels. I point to the rubber duck and say "duck," and my daughter repeats. Probably she's imitating the sounds she hears from adults so she can get an approving smile or a more tangible reward, like a lollipop. It takes some time before a child is ready to speak in the indicative.

The notion that words are mainly intended to communicate thoughts treats language as if it were off on the sidelines, observing the world from outside, waiting for us to pick up labels to attach to things and events in the world. But our language doesn't describe the world from the outside. We're not spectators of the world. We're agents and actors, and our language is one of the main tools we use to "agent" and to act. We're in the world, and we're the users of language, so our language is in the world too.

By this point in the book, you know the next step in this dance: if language is in the world, then the world is also in language. You know that I'm going to say that the contours of language match the contours of time, and the subtle contours of erotic love, and of human relationships, and of our relationship to the world. And I *am* going to say just that. I'm very predictable. I do believe that language necessarily stands in a relation to the world, and that it would not be language without this relationship. And I believe that the relationship of language to the world, and the relationship of one part of language to another, is a relationship of mutual indwelling. Words leave their mark on other words; traces of prior texts mark each new text; the world inhabits the word just as much as word inhabits world. And we wouldn't have language at all if all these were not true.

How? Much in every way.

Metonymy is a way of naming something by referring to something closely associated with it. "The crown said" is a classic example. In most universes, including ours, crowns do not actually speak, but since the crown is associated with the king or queen, we can name the crown as a way of naming the entire apparatus of monarchy. "White houses" don't literally report or respond, but journalists commonly speak as if at least one White House does. Absent the history and usage and institutional context of these metonymies, they are nonsensical. Assuming he knows the English language, what is an Amazonian tribesman to make of our belief that crowns and houses make announcements? He might think it's nothing but high-tech shamanism and sophisticated mumbo jumbo. Metonymy is meaningful only because of historical, political, and cultural contexts. The world is taken up into and transforms our language, as language indwells and remakes the world.

Even when I write or speak more literally, I take the world into language. Once I call something a "swan," the bird I call a swan *is* a swan. I've brought the bird to speech; the bird has been translated into the sound "swan." My interaction with the bird itself is shaped by what I call it. For English speakers, swans become swannish, and things that are similar to swans (a tall, elegant model on the catwalk) also come to be swannish. Language is not a picture of the world standing over against the world. It's in the world, and whenever we talk about the world, the world comes to dwell in language.

The history and usage of the word "swan" are mysteriously contained within the word. If someone sees a swan for the first time, he sees only a brilliantly white bird with an elegant neck skimming across a pond. If he is told "That's a swan," he has a label and not much more. Next time he sees one, he will know what to call it. But suppose that he has grown up in a typical English-speaking home, has heard about the ugly duckling and the swan princess and perhaps knows that swan is an old English holiday delicacy and that the queen of England owns all the mute swans that live in open water in Britain. Suppose that, despite having a store of knowledge about swans, he has never seen one or a picture of one. In this case, teaching him the name "swan" is more than teaching him a label. All the lore and law and legend associated with swans come into play. The word contains in some fashion the history of its usage. That's why you can hardly utter the word "swan" to an English speaker without unleashing a flood of associations in that person's mind.

Even words that are essentially synonyms mean somewhat different things because of their history. If you call someone a "pig," you condemn the person as a greedy glutton. Calling someone a "swine" suggests something altogether more vicious, even savage. Dictionaries tell us that the words mean the same thing, but because of the different historical usage of each they create a different impact. "Rats" and "mice" are closely related rodents, but the connotations of the two are quite different. Call someone a "mouse," and you're charging the person with timidity and weakness. Call someone a "rat" and you are charging the person with a particularly slimy form of vice. The actual uses of the word by actual speakers and writers dwell in language and affect what words mean.

Most of the time, we don't think much about word derivations or histories. We don't think about the medieval Latin roots of "rock," or the source of the word "swan." But poets are different from the rest of us. They remind us of older, forgotten meanings of words, and the family connections of one word with another. Even in everyday conversation, there will nearly always be a punster nearby who will call attention to the overlaps and interpenetrations of words. "Duck" (the bird) and "duck!" (a protective action) don't have any historical connection. It's an accident of English that we have two such diverse meanings for the same sound. Yet once that accident is embedded in the language, it opens up possibilities of meaning that wouldn't have been available otherwise. We all know wise guys who respond to the warning "Duck!" with something like "Mallard?" or "Quack."

If language weren't an item in the world, an available tool for understanding and acting, it wouldn't be language as we know it. On the other hand, if the world didn't get incorporated into our language, it would be useless. Without this mutual indwelling, language would not exist at all—just as I wouldn't exist without being in a relation of mutual penetration with the world, just as humans wouldn't be who they are without others inhabiting them and them inhabiting others, just as sex wouldn't be sex or love be love without a union in difference, just as time is time as we know it only because the past and future inhabit a present that also inhabits them. In each case, things aren't what they are unless they are Möbius shaped, unless they curved into others and then curved back on themselves, unless the inside were the outside and the outside the inside, unless things that are utterly distinct were at the same time strangely twisted and tangled into one.

I'm still wondering if we asked the right question back at the beginning of this chapter. I asked how "marks and pixels and vibrations" communicate thoughts, and I've answered by saying that "communicating thoughts" is not the only thing language does. But I wonder if I was right to describe language as "marks and pixels and vibrations." I'm beginning to think I wasn't.

In his treatise "On the Teacher" (*De magistro*), Augustine puzzled over the question of how language can communicate anything new. He pointed out that we can't know the meaning of a word without knowing something about the thing that the word names. I don't know what "Tasmanian devil" means unless I know what a Tasmanian devil is. But if I know the thing before someone names it, I haven't learned anything new when I learn the name. I've only picked up a label to attach to the crazy little critter. I have to know the thing in order to know the sign, so the sign doesn't teach me. If the sign awakens some idea that is already in me, the idea must have already been there in my mind in a dormant state, so again I haven't really learned anything. Yet we *do* use language to teach, and it seems that we actually do learn new things by means of language. Augustine solved this puzzle by citing a Bible verse: "There is only one teacher," Jesus said (see Matt. 23:8). Augustine took Jesus quite literally and said that we learn because we are taught by the "interior teacher" who is God. We aren't really taught through signs at all. God illumines our minds so that we can know.

Augustine may have been right that we can't unravel the mystery of language without talking about God, but he underplays the role of human language in the process of learning. I don't know much about Chinese history, but what I do know came almost entirely through language. The handful of pictures and artifacts I've seen wouldn't make much sense to me without explanation. We know many things that we neither have direct experience of nor ever will, and language is invariably a part of coming to know them. I didn't have an idea of the "Ming Dynasty" embedded in my brain before someone or some book taught me about it.[6]

I've even learned a thing or two in the process of writing the first half of this chapter. I knew when I began that I would be writing about language, but I hadn't planned out each step of the chapter. I used the word "duck" to explain how words convey warnings and commands and not simply ideas and facts, and then I used the word "duck" in a different sense to illustrate another point. I knew that the word "duck" was ambiguous before I started the chapter, but I didn't plan to highlight that ambiguity when I started writing. Think how often you have learned things from your own speaking and writing, not to mention the speaking and writing of other people.[7]

Two false assumptions are often made about language, and Augustine isn't free of them. The first is that language is a matter of assigning labels to things. At the park we spot a duck swimming lazily in the pond, and we assign the sound "duck" to that object, so we can make a report when we get back home about the waterfowl that we spotted. Words are not just labels for things, a point that can be illustrated by thinking about the words in the first clause of this sentence. "Words" and "labels" and "things" are all things to which we assign these labels. But what is the "thing" named by "are" or "not" or "just" or "for"? Even if we say that the words are signs of ideas, what sort of idea is signified by "just" in the clause above? If we think that all words are labels—that every word is a kind of noun—then we're headed for some difficulties. What is called "nominalization" not only distorts what language is but also leads into other blind alleys.[8]

The other assumption has to do with the relationship between physical signs (sounds or marks) and the ideas, facts, feelings, or instructions they convey. Thinkers often betray a veiled desire to peel back the sensible features of language, the sounds and the visible signs, in order to get to the naked reality of pure language. This has deep roots in Western thought, one of the roots being the Platonic preference for the intelligible over the sensible. Ideas are more real than sensible things, since sensible things are shadowy copies of the *really* real things, which are known only to the intellect. Because he begins with this sort of assumption, Augustine has a hard time with the notion that

71

sounds and marks might themselves be carriers of ideas. If ideas are going to be conveyed *purely*, they are best conveyed in a purely intellectual way. Sensible signs intrude and distort. The sensible features of language are a form of static that makes it harder for us to hear ideas. O that we could communicate ideas without the distorting effects of words!

Common as this view is, it's obviously an error. Take a scalpel and scrape the ink off this page: Will you find out what I *really* think? Plug your ears so you can't hear your wife or husband talking to you: Does the resulting silence give you a clearer idea of what he or she is saying? Hardly. If you try that little experiment, you have some unpleasant days ahead of you.

If I say, "I have a knock-down argument for the existence of God," you'll want to hear it. And if I say, "No, sorry, speaking or writing the argument would contaminate it," you'll suspect that in fact I have no argument at all. And I don't, not really. I can bat ideas around in my head, and that is an argument of sorts. But arguments exist to contend for the truth and to convince *others* of the truth, or at least to test the truth. Philosophy and science and all other forms of inquiry are *social* institutions, depending on interactions with other people. An argument has to be thrown out in front of other people so that those pros and cons can be made clear. If I were a bugger from *Ender's Game*, I could throw arguments out in front of other people without using words. But I'm not a bugger, and I'm operating on the assumption that you aren't one either. Arguments need to be put into language so that other people can consider and respond.

If you strip away the sensible features of language, you're not left with pure language. You're left with pure nothing.[9]

It works the other way too (you knew I would say that). If I write (as I'm about to do!), "Gmborsh jappblv qpioad," you won't know what I'm saying. You can see the letters, and you might, with some difficulty, sound out the words. The letters are visible and are associated with sounds. The "words" of the "sentence" have sensible qualities. But they have no meaning because they aren't part of any human language. So language can't get by with just the sensible qualities alone.

As my identity is formed by the "indwelling" of others in me, as sexual union is mutual penetration and inhabitation, as time is the interpenetration of the past and future in the present, so language is a complex, an entangled union of sensible and intellectual. The intellectual and sensible qualities of language aren't interchangeable. Each is irreducibly itself, but neither can do what language does without the other. Nonsense sounds communicate no sense; sense without sound or marks doesn't communicate at all. The intellectual inhabits the sensible, and the sensible is housed in the intellectual; meaning indwells the sensible sounds and the sounds curve and twine and curl around meanings. This is not a matter of balancing two things that are opposed to each other, two things that might exist without the other. It's more like recognizing that there is no inside to a house without an outside. You don't *balance* inside and outside. You don't have to balance them, because neither can possibly be at all without the other. Language is more like a Möbius strip in which inside and outside form a continuum. Sense and sound, sense and marking, fold back on each other. Ideas penetrate sounds and marks. Marks and sounds depend on the housing of ideas to make them meaningful. So I was wrong to speak of language as "marks and pixels and vibrations." Language is "marks and pixels and vibrations that *bear sense*," or it is "*sense inhabiting* marks and pixels and vibrations."

Augustine's puzzlement over the ability of language to teach arises from his reduction of language to signs. The question, How can language communicate what we don't already know? assumes that language is mere sense and not intellect. It reduces to the question, How can sounds or marks communicate truth? The answer is that they don't, because language is not just sounds and marks but *significant* sounds and marks. Once we

73

get that right, the question dissolves. Asking how meaningful sounds and marks can teach us is hardly worth the trouble of asking, because meaningful sounds and marks obviously bear meaning. If meaningful signs cannot teach, nothing can.

Forgetfulness of this interweaving of sense and sensibility has continued to the present. Over the past century, linguists have assumed that the signs (the "signifier") that we use to signify concepts (the "signified") are arbitrary.[10] But this is the result of a confusion.[11] Our minds aren't full of empty memories of sounds that have no concepts attached, nor of concepts that have no names. We might occasionally find a stray unattached name floating around in our brain, a verbal bar-hopper trying to pick up sense. We might sense the vague outlines of a concept that we can't yet put into words. Neither of these, though, is language, and in the main, our minds are full of *named* concepts, concepts with sounds and signs already attached to them, attached so inseparably that we cannot call up the concepts without the name. We learn the name-concept together, whether it's the name-concept of duck, or of justice, or of the ancient city Alexandria. If we don't have a one-word label, at least we can embody our concepts with a sentence or two. The relation between signifier and concept could be "arbitrary" only if the two were separate realities, only if the concept existed prior to the signifier being attached to it. Since concepts and signifiers indwell one another, neither exists without the other. Neither *can* exist without the other, and language itself cannot exist without this mutual indwelling.

Confusion arises because a third factor gets smuggled into the discussion alongside the signifier and the signified, the thing itself. Words seem to be arbitrary labels when we're comparing names and *things*, rather than names and concepts. And it's true the things of the world don't come with preassigned labels. Cows don't have the word "cow" (not to mention *vache* or *Kuh* or *koe*) branded on their haunches at birth. But saying that the relation between names and *things* is arbitrary is very different from saying that the relation of names and *concepts* is arbitrary. Names and concepts form an inseparable union. As Emile Benveniste puts it, "The signifier and the signified . . . make up the ensemble as the embodier and the embodiment. The signifier is the phonic translation of a concept; the signified is the mental counterpart of the signifier." The concept indwells the visual or audible sign; the sign "overlies and commands" the concept.[12]

It's not even entirely true to say that the relation of name and *thing* is arbitrary. Languages develop over time, and people make choices about what to call things. The original choices at the dark dawn of a language are more or less arbitrary: Why should the sound *be* mean "be," or the sound *bee* mean "bee"? There is nothing inherently rocky about "rocks," nothing swannish about "swans," nothing inherently flowery about the word "flower." Sometime in the distant past, someone assigned labels more or less randomly to things, and that choice was reinforced by the consensus of a community and the usage of years. This is obvious from the fact that groups assign different labels to things. For French speakers, rocks aren't rocky because they aren't rocks but *roches*. To the degree that humans speaking different languages assign different names to things, the names are arbitrary.

Once language gets off the ground, though, the choices are not arbitrary at all. "Rock" and *roche* are not the same word, but they are clearly related, both derived from the medieval Latin word *rocca*. The German *Schwan* and the English "swan" are connected, the product of a long journey through Saxon, Dutch, Norse, and Old German. Not only are new words borrowed from other languages, but new words are often formed by combining elements existing in the language as well. "Microscope" is hardly an arbitrary term, since it hearkens back to two Greek terms, *micro* ("small") and *skopein* ("to see"). Other words are formed on the basis of puns and analogies between different words, both in the language itself and from other languages.[13] Words are in the world, and the world is in the word. Our words are not arbitrary because they incarnate a verbal history.

Since we all speak languages that have already gotten off the ground, the "arbitrariness" of the relation of words and things isn't a practical issue. None of us is inventing a new language. We might make up new words, but those aren't going to be arbitrary. We'll borrow from existing words, or from our personal experience, or from history. "Google" has connotations today that it didn't have thirty years ago, but it was originally derived from the mathematical term "googol," which is the number one with a hundred zeroes after it.

We don't speak isolated, individual words. Most often, we speak and write sequences of words. As Augustine recognized, the mystery of language is one dimension of the mystery of time. Spoken language exists and then dies, like the present moment. A sentence makes sense only if the earlier words of the sentence are retained as the later words come to be spoken. Only if the first words continue to live on in memory and to indwell the later words do the first words make their sense. Past indwells the present; future indwells the present. And without this mutual indwelling of first words and last words, there is no sentence. Each word struts and frets its moment on the stage, and then humbly yields to the next. If the word is a ham who tries to steal the show, it will drown out all the words that follow, and nothing will make sense. But it can't leave the stage either, because without it the rest of the players' speeches are contextless sound and fury, signifying nothing. Each word has to make space for the next and the next in succession. As the sentence performs, each word becomes a home to, and makes its home in, every other.

Metaphor is a figure of speech that speaks of one thing in terms of another thing. "Life is a journey" or "Life is a zoo" are metaphors in this sense. More subtly, a writer implies a meta-phorical relationship between this and that without stating it straightforwardly. "Before I met my husband, I'd never fallen in love. I'd stepped in it a few times," says Rita Rudner. The meta-phorical comparison is between love and—what?—a puddle or a vat into which one might fall. The metaphoricity is multiple here, because the phrase "stepped in it" usually has a negative connotation in contemporary English. When you refer to stepping in *it*, people generally understand that you are omitting an initial *sh*. The metaphor shifts without warning: to fall in love is to fall into—what?—a delicious chocolate pie? But that *felix culpa* was preceded by some bad love affairs, pictured as a pile of manure.

Language itself is a species of metaphor.[14] "What's that?" you ask. And I say, "That's a swan" or "That's a duck." Well, not exactly. The bird swimming elegantly on the pond is *not* the sound "swan," nor is the creature awkwardly waddling across the yard the sound "duck." The "is" in "That *is* a swan" is already metaphorical, because the sound is not identical to the thing.

The propriety of metaphor depends on the mutual indwelling of word in word, and of world in word. Rudner's metaphor, and the humor of it, works because we can conceive of love as something we "fall" into, and because "falling in" and "stepping in" have multiple meanings, so that when she says *x* she says *y* at the same time, even though she doesn't actually say *y* at all. A second sense is implied by the words that are said, a second sense that echoes around the words that are actually spoken. She can say two things at the same time because the words she speaks contain other words, implying meanings that are never stated. If word didn't indwell word, then the use of metaphor would be a power play; Rudner would be using one word to beat another word into submission. But if words indwell words, and if things and words are mutually indwelling, then metaphor is not imposed from outside but a revelation of the character of language, the intimate interpenetration of one word by others.

77

Metaphors are an intensified form of verbal indwelling, with an expected meaning and the unexpected meaning inhabiting the same words.

Metaphor is arguably not just a linguistic figure, but inherent in the way we conceptualize the world. We cannot do without metaphor; metaphor is not just language, but the structure of the way we think. Metaphor is cognitive and not merely linguistic.[15] We navigate our experience using basic metaphors. Up and down are metaphors for advance and growth, or decline and contraction. Life is a journey with a beginning, a winding way, and a destination. Argument is war. We extrapolate various other metaphors from the base metaphor. Because argument is war, we strategize our arguments, attack and retreat, protect our flank. It's not simply that language is characterized by this feature of mutual indwelling. It's the pattern of thought itself.

Even more strongly, we can say that the analogies that metaphors identify are actually *there* in the world. When I say that argument is war, I am neither tying argument up in a military straitjacket nor revealing the metaphorical contours of the mind, but uncovering something that is really true about the world. There really *is* something warlike about argument, or argumentative about war; there's a war hidden in argument or an argument housed within every war. When my heart turns to love, I begin to see what is actually there—that roses are like love, that love is a journey. When I talk about the body politic I'm not engaged in flights of political fancy, since political entities do function like bodies, and bodies like political entities, with the stomach feeding all the rest of the members. Bad fortune is in fact full of slings and arrows, as slings and arrows are certainly a form of bad fortune.

This strong form of my argument makes sense in the light of the previous chapters. After all, my claim from the beginning has been that mutual penetration is not something imposed on the world but the basic pattern of reality. It is not a projection from my brain, but ontological, a form entwined in the very being of all that is, in the very being of beings and of being. Or, better, it is the hardwiring of creatures and of creation. If that's the case, might we hope to learn that it is hardwired into whatever is responsible for the being of beings and of being, for the creation of creatures and of creation? Might we hope that the rediscovery of the same is a trace of *something*? I believe we might hope so, but we will put that to the side until later. We aren't finished exploring language yet, and we still have some other thickets to cut through.

However strongly we try to make the case, metaphor depends on the very pattern that is the focus of this book. Words differ. Words have unique properties, both empirically (sound, visible features) and semantically. Yet these irreducibly different words do what they do only because they inhabit one another. Words contain other words, even as they are contained by words. Things contain other things even as they are contained by those things.

If we zoom out to consider larger units of language, the point becomes even more obvious. If we think of texts instead of words, it becomes clear that texts mutually contain and condition each other. As alert (and probably unemployed) lit majors will have already noticed, I alluded to several Shakespeare plays in the past several paragraphs. Those strutting, fretting, furious, and sounding words are from *Macbeth*. As I wrote that extended reference to the body politic and the stomach of that body, I was thinking of Menenius's speech in the first scene of *Coriolanus*, where the old senator condemns the plebs of Rome for not honoring the patrician "stomach" that feeds them. "Slings and arrows" is of course found in Hamlet's soliloquy. Those texts "indwell" my text, Shakespeare's words inhabiting my words, his phrases interspersed with my own, his sentences weaving in and out of sentences that I've composed.

Does my text also "indwell" Shakespeare's? Not in the same fashion. I'm writing centuries after Shakespeare finished his

plays, so Will couldn't allude to *my* writing even if he wanted
to. In a more attenuated sense, I have added something to Shakespeare's plays by placing them in a new context.

Literary texts depend on this pattern of indwelling. Many
millennia ago, someone wrote the story of Abraham and Isaac
in the book of Genesis. Abraham was commanded to sacrifice
his son, and dutifully followed God's command. Others have
told the story again and again since: Philo took Genesis into his
De Abrahamo; the early Christians found an allegory of Jesus in
the story of Abraham and Isaac; Calvin's successor in Geneva,
Theodore Beza, wrote *A Tragedie of Abrahams Sacrifice*; in *Tess
of the d'Urbervilles*, Thomas Hardy has his Mr. Clare mourn
for his son "as Abraham might have mourned over the doomed
Isaac while they went up the hill together."[16] Kierkegaard wrote
a long meditation on the story in *Fear and Trembling*, deriving
from it a religious principle that involves a "teleological suspen-
sion of the ethical." All of these texts are indwelled by the text
of Genesis, and each of them enriches the original text.[17] The
indwelling of one text by another is not ornamental or "*merely
literary.*" Without the prior texts, the new text wouldn't exist.
Kierkegaard wouldn't have written *Fear and Trembling* if he had
never read Genesis, but, more significantly, *Fear and Trembling*
would make no sense as a text without the indwelling presence
of Genesis 22. Unless a set of words makes sense, it is not a text,
and the set of words in these texts makes sense only because and
insofar as *another* text has taken up residence in it. Without this
interweaving and interleaving of text and text, there is no text.

I've said it again and again. I don't think you're dense, but
I am, and I need to keep saying it to help *me* remember what a
wondrous design we've discovered. I keep saying it because I'm
amazed at the world's maze. So I'll say it again: language, like
my relation to the world, like human relations and especially
erotic relationships, like time, like all these, language is what it
is by virtue of this enigmatic quality of reciprocal habitation,

this delicate rhythm of mutual penetration, of pouring out and pouring in, of enveloping the very thing that envelops. Language exists and does what it does only because the irreducibly different words and sentences and texts dwell in other words and sentences. If we see it in all these dimensions of our existence, we hope that we will see more of it when we get to the next terrace. See it, or *hear* it. Music, I think I hear music.

6

Chords

You've been reading for a while. It's time to break the monotony. Let's start this chapter with some experiments.

The first comes in three steps. Look up from the book. Locate the person nearest you. Shout. (What you shout doesn't matter, so long as it's loud.) Then play the scientist and objectively observe the results. Unless the person nearest you is deaf or dead or inhumanly self-controlled, he or she will likely jump a little and look at you with an expression somewhere in the neighborhood of quizzicality and anger.

You've demonstrated one feature of sound: sound signals across space. Like your nose and eyes, your ears can receive messages from a distance. Some things you hear come to you from a great distance, as we count off the seconds between the lightning bolt and the resulting thunderclap.

That was simple enough. Let's try another, similar to the last. Stand and walk out of the room so that the nearest person can't see you. Then shout. Provided the person nearest you is still alive and still capable of hearing, he or she will again react, this time with annoyance. "What *do* you want? What *are* you reading?"

This time you have identified a feature of the sense of hearing that it shares only with smell. In order to see an object, you need to have a clear line of sight. You can see only what is immediately present to you.[1] It's different with sound. Like aromas, sounds communicate even in absence. If you get far enough away or put enough walls and barriers between you, you will lose the ability to communicate by sound. But if your vocal chords are strong enough, you can shout loudly enough to be heard by the neighbors. I don't recommend shouting that loudly; that's not part of the experiment. But you could if you wanted to try it, because sound is a presence in absence.

This is entertaining. Let's try another experiment, similar to the second. Turn on some music. Stand in the center of the room and listen for a moment. Turn around slowly and listen. Walk to a corner of the room and listen. Walk to the opposite corner of the room and listen. Lie down on the floor and listen. So long as your mother or spouse or some other authority figure isn't looking, step onto a chair and listen. Walk to the next room and repeat the experiment. Keep moving from room to room until you can't hear the music anymore.

If you have a good ear, you might hear slight variations in the sound at different points in the room and from different orientations. For the most part you will hear the same music playing in every part of the space you are in. The sound has a source: your iPod or your computer or your phonograph or your personal string quartet. But from that source, sound diffuses to fill the available space. You don't have to be turned toward the source to hear it. The music is up to the ceiling and down to the floor, in the center of the room and all the way to each corner, and then into the next room too. *All* the music is *everywhere* in the space as long as the music keeps playing.[2]

This is exceedingly odd. You have to be turned toward the source of the music to *see* it, and even when you see it, you *never* see all of it. What strikes your eye is one facet of the computer or iPod, one perspective on the object. When you look at the front, you can't see the back. You can walk around the back of the computer, but as soon as you do you lose the sight of the front. You can see back and front together, sort of, if you look at the object from above, but in fact you are again seeing the object from only one angle. If you dart back and forth from the front to the back, a Cubist image will emerge and you'll probably gets breathless and dizzy. I don't doubt your computer has both a front and a back. If you have doubts, you can confirm with another experiment: Put a video camera in front of your computer and then walk to the back. As you expected, the front stays where it was when you move. (You can do the same more cheaply with a mirror.) Without that kind of technological enhancement, you can never see more than one surface of an object at a time. We *imagine* that there are three dimensions to the objects we see, but we don't actually see those dimensions at the same time.

"Seeing is believing," we say, meaning that "I won't believe *x* until I see it with my own eyes." More realistically, "seeing is believing" in a very different sense: when we say "I see the computer" we more literally mean "I see one surface of the computer and I am confident that the rest is there too." To say "I see it" is to make a confession of faith.

As our experiment has proved, this isn't true of sound. We hear sounds whole, even very complex ones like one of the moments in a Prokofiev piano concerto. And we can hear these complex sounds even if the source of the sound is not within eyeshot, even if, like the castaways on Prospero's land or Rosencrantz (or is it Guildenstern?), we hear music but don't know the source. We might say that this is because sound is one-dimensional, existing only in time and not in height, depth, and breadth. Technically that may be true, but we've already seen that sound does fill space and we use spatial metaphors to describe the experience of music. Music goes up and down and moves along slowly or rapidly toward its resting place, or so we say. Whether one-dimensional or not, sound provides the miracle of presence in absence. It also offers the miracle of miracles of *total* presence in absence. *All* of the music is *everywhere*.

Your experiments have proved something else. You can walk around the room *through* the sound. Vibrating air molecules do strike you, but they are so nearly massless that you don't feel them unless you crank the music way way *way* up. Even then, you can walk freely through the music, though the woofers might make your hair waft a little. Music envelops you. It totally surrounds you in every bit of the space of the room, but it doesn't imprison you. If you need a comparison, try walking through the nearest wall and you'll quickly notice that aural and visible objects are quite different in this regard.[3] Sound fills space without taking up space. It proudly occupies the room but at the same time humbly yields the space entirely to whatever else is there. Music and musical space are related as I am to the world, as fathers are to sons, as lovers are to one another, as words are to the other words around them in the sentences they inhabit. Music fills its space, yet musical space is filled by all sorts of other things at the same time.

"Is it not strange that sheep's gut can hale souls out of men's bodies?" asks Benedick in Shakespeare's *Much Ado about Nothing*. Strange it is, but this strange thing is true. Sheep gut stretched into strings makes music that enters you. It extracts the soul from the body so that your soul feels as if it *is* the lark ascending, the flowing Moldau, the *Heiliger Dankgesang* after recovery from an illness. Few things are more deeply meaningful to people than the music they listen to. Few experiences touch our hearts like hearing a piece of music. It happened to me in King's College Chapel. I had gone to hear the Cambridge Singers' performance of Tallis's *Spem in Alium*, but it was Allegri's *Miserere* that transported me. To this day, I can't listen to Allegri's setting of Psalm 51 without hearing the soprano burst through the ribbed vault of the chapel to reach toward heaven. The music that was all around me in all its totality also entered the depths of my soul. It is always so: we envelop the sound that envelops us. The sound is simultaneously in, with, and under us.

One final experiment: keep that music playing, and listen carefully to the notes. In most of the music you listen to, you'll hear chords, two or more notes played at the same time. You can get the same effect by going to the nearest piano and striking several notes simultaneously. You'll hear a chord, though it may be a dissonant one if you didn't plan what you were going to play ahead of time. Listen intently to that chord and ask yourself if you can tell where one note ends and the other begins. It will be impossible. Each note occupies the same soundscape at the same time, and each note occupies the soundscape as fully as the other. Each note occupies the whole sound space, and each note occupies the other notes that are being played.

You can't hear it as clearly, but you get the same effect by striking a single note. A C is a chord to itself, since alongside the vibrations that make the string or horn sound C there is a series of vibrations that create half-heard overtones. Because the C note is the one sounded, it's the most obvious note, but the others are sounding around and within it. Given the nature of the physics of sound, you can't sound a C note without other notes playing alongside it. Those other tones are part of what make up the sound "C." C would not be C without the other sounds.

A chord is overtones on top of overtones. When you play two notes at the same time, each has its own set of overtones, which join together occupying the same "space," each providing a musical setting for each of the others. Overtones of overtones constitute the overall sound of a note. Mysteriously, notes that are not played provide part of the sound we hear. In short, not only chords but even individual notes are complexes of sounds that all occupy the same space and interpenetrate each other at the same time. The theologian Jeremy Begbie writes,

> When more than one sound is present, occupying the same space while remaining audibly distinct, we may speak of a space not of mutual exclusion but of "interpenetration." Sounds do not have to "cut each other off" or obscure each other, in the manner of visually perceived objects. The tones of a chord can be heard sounding *through* each other. In the acoustic realm, in other words, there is no neat distinction between a place and its occupant. . . . Music directly "pulls the strings," so to speak, of the spatial framework in which it is deployed—no neat divide marks off occupant and place in musical experience. We need only to think of a three-tone major chord, which we hear as three distinct, mutually enhancing (not mutually exclusive) sounds, but together occupying the same aural space.[4]

Sounds occupy the space created by other sounds, and in occupying that space also create space for the sounds in which they exist. Each envelops each; each envelops the sounds it it is enveloped by.

You can draw the same conclusion by listening to a sequence of notes, especially if you are able to play them slowly. What we hear in music is not one note at a time, each discrete and isolated in itself. Each note leans ahead toward the next note. Each note creates an expectation of a following note. As Victor Zuckerkandl has put it, a line of music is "always *between* tones, *on the way* from one tone to another; our hearing does not remain with the tone, it reaches through it and beyond it."[5] You can't get rid of the individual notes. Without them, you won't have any music at all. Each note is irreducibly itself, with its own frequency of vibration and its own proliferation of overtones. But notes are not self-standing atoms of sound. They resemble "pure betweenness, pure passing over."[6] Even when notes are not played at the same time, they require each other. The C in the C scale leans ahead to the D. The penultimate chord of the hymn leaves us expecting the tonic and we are unsatisfied and slightly confused if that resolution never arrives.

You'll notice that we've moved from experiments with sound to experiments with music. That was deliberate. I wanted to show the continuity between the qualities of sound per se and the qualities of the organized sound that constitutes music. Examining both sounds and music has again brought to the fore the pattern we have discovered again and again in this book: sounds (notes), like moments of time and objects, are not *only* irreducible things unto themselves but exist in relations and sequences that are essential to the uniquely individual sound. Sound and music bring out this quality even more clearly than other phenomena of the world. More than solid objects, more than human relationships, more than the reciprocal penetration of times, more than the interlocking of distinct words, music exhibits the pattern of "mutual interpenetration" that marks all reality.

I wanted to talk about music because people have long considered music not just one phenomenon among many but as the secret key to understanding the whole of reality. Pythagoreans are known for their belief that mathematics is the language of the world. For the Pythagoreans, this insight had a mystical character. Numbers were quasi-divine entities. Strip off the mysticism, though, and the Pythagorean view of numbers is very much our modern view. With the formulation of calculus and more recent mathematical disciplines, we are even able to describe movement and apparently random activity in the world mathematically. Using ones and zeroes and electronics, our computing machines can perform incredibly complicated operations and can communicate with someone on the other side of the planet or view pictures from a telescope in deep space. We are not Pythagoreans, but we still act on the belief that the world is in some fundamental sense numerical.

Legend has it that Pythagoras one day walked past a blacksmith's shop where the blacksmiths were pounding their anvils. He thought the sound beautiful, and when he examined the hammers, he discovered that the hammer lengths were proportionate to each other, the second hammer half the size of the first and the third hammer two-thirds the size of the first. From this, Pythagoras learned the principles of harmony and the mathematical key to musical scales.

The story is apocryphal. Hammers don't produce harmonies in the way that strings and columns of air do. But the story accurately reflects the Pythagorean obsession with music, which they extended beyond the experiments that proved the mathematical qualities of notes and harmonies. Because they believed that the universe was mathematical, and because they believed that music was mathematically organized, they naturally came to the conclusion that the universe was also musically organized. Pythagoreans invented the notion of the "harmony of the spheres," the idea that the planets move in relation to one another in proportions that correspond to musical proportions and produce a symphony in the heavens. Music is not only an art. It is a clue to the cosmos.

The idea has had a good run. Plato claimed that the "twin" sciences of music and astronomy appeal to the ear and eye respectively: "As the eyes, said I, seem formed for studying astronomy, so do the ears seem formed for harmonious motions: and these seem to be twin sciences to one another, as also the Pythagoreans say."[7] Cicero, Pliny, and Ptolemy all made use of the concept, and it was taken up by Christian thinkers into the Middle Ages. As a young convert, Augustine wrote the treatise *De musica* in a Platonic vein, and Boethius followed in the century after Augustine with his own *De musica*, in which he identified three forms of music: *musica mundana* (harmony of the spheres), *musica humana* (harmony between body and soul in the human), and *musica instrumentalis* (music made by musical instruments). Human beings are microcosms, small models of the world, insofar as we reflect the harmonies of the universe itself in the harmonious proportions of our lives. Dante thought of outer space as a series of glassy spheres containing planets and other heavenly bodies, rotating and rubbing against each other to produce exquisite celestial music. The notion wasn't dropped out in the modern world. Some of the founders of modern science—Copernicus, the young Galileo, Kepler, Newton—were inspired by the notion of what Kepler called "the harmony of the world."[8]

I'm not an advocate for any particular version of the harmony of the spheres. My point is only to note (ha!) that many thinkers have considered music a clue to the mysteries of the universe and of human life. That, I believe, is an eminently sound (ha!) intuition, provided that we keep in mind the qualities of sound and music that our earlier experiments revealed to us.

As Begbie has observed, music shows that fixity and order are not identical.[9] When we use metaphors drawn from visible reality, we think of order as immobility. A pyramid or a ziggurat is the architectural icon of order, the single king or the god at the pinnacle, supported below by his court, his nobles, his armies, his citizens, and finally, crushed beneath the weight of the structure, his slaves. Music obviously does not possess order of this sort. Chords and sounds in music may stay still for a few moments, but even when they stay still they are still alive with constant vibration. And music typically doesn't stay still for very long. It is always in motion; it *is* motion, but not chaotic or disorderly motion. It represents a radically different sort of order than the sculptural or the architectural. Music gives, in Zuckerkandl's words, "an order in what is wholly flux, of a building without matter."[10]

Augustine and many others recognized that music offers special insights into the nature of time. Music reveals that subjection to time is not an obstacle to human life but the condition of human flourishing. This goes against the grain of some of our common intuitions. We feel that time imprisons us. We fail or sin, and as soon as it's done it's too late to undo. We come to the sickening realization that we have not loved our children or our spouse as we ought, but the very form of our regret, that perfect tense "have . . . loved," means that it's too late to change it. We hope for something so intensely that we can touch it, but we have to slog through unproductive moment after unproductive moment until what we hope for comes to pass.

Affirming the goodness of time certainly violates some of the basic principles of religion and philosophy through the ages. As we noted in chapter 4, for many philosophers time was a problem to be explained or explained away, the prison that had to be escaped. For some Greek philosophers, the world of change—that is, the world of time—cannot be ultimately real. To be ultimately real, something has to be static, ever itself, not turning into something else, not aging or decaying. Only the forms are truly real, and they are truly real precisely because they are impervious to time's changes. Religions often display the same impulse.

Visual arts—painting and sculpture and to some extent architecture—embody this aspiration to transcend time. It takes time to absorb the full significance of a painting, but we can get the gist in a moment: Ah, yes, Van Gogh's bandaged ear, the pathos of Titian's *Pietà*, Magritte's pipe that is not a pipe, the carnage of *Guernica*. It's impossible, though, to take in music in a moment. You can take in a few notes, a few chords, a few lyrics more or less instantaneously, but those notes or chords do not make a musical piece. You can only perceive the music by waiting and listening, but when we wait we find that glories are in store, not only at the end, but all through the process of listening. Music forces time upon us, but shows us that the passage of time and the patience it demands are gifts to be received rather than evils to be endured. Music demonstrates, as Rowan Williams has put it, that "there are things you will learn only by passing through this process, by being caught up in this series of relations and transformations."[11] Time demands patient waiting, and thus living in time is a way to maturity. The attempt to bypass time, even if it's done by a sophisticated philosopher or artist, is infantile.

Because it is temporal, music depends on transience, as does language. Both manifest the mystery of time, whose moments must yield to and make room for one another if there is to be time at all. Augustine pointed out that in a speech words fade out as other words follow on their heels. This isn't some unfortunate, tragic condition. It is necessary to deliver a meaningful speech at all. If each word stood its ground and refused to yield, word would pile up on word and soon you'd have a pileup of historic proportions. Nothing would make sense. You can't take in even the few dozen words of the Gettysburg Address all at once. Words have to occupy the stage for a moment, and then move backstage as the spotlight shines on the next word. Music is beautiful and meaningful in the same way. As Begbie says, "Music depends heavily for its meaning on finitude at every level. Tones give way to tones. Music is constantly dying, giving way." But transience doesn't make music futile; music has its integrity, beauty, order, glory "in and through this very transience."[12] Musical notes have to withdraw and make room for one another for there to be music at all. If they refuse to fade to memory, the sound will be cacophonous rather than harmonic or melodic.

Like music, Begbie points out, time has different qualities: "different rates at which things happen, different concentrations of activities at different periods. . . . Plants and animals possess different rates of change and flourish at different points relative to their birth and death. People 'reach their peak' at different stages." This is not a sign of corruption but rather is "intrinsically bound up with the constitution of entities themselves and intended for good." At every moment in a piece of music, a multitude of things is going on. The rhythmic pattern overlaps with and penetrates the melodic pattern; the melodic pattern overlaps with and penetrates the overall structure of the piece. Each aspect of the music sets the context for the others, and none of them is more "fundamental" than the others. It's not as if the melodic pattern is the real music and the rhythm a secondary addition. There is no melodic pattern without rhythm, nor vice versa. And this overlapping and interpenetrating quality is one of the ways that music points to the mysteries of the world, for time has precisely this layered musical quality, different rhythms folding into and over one another to make the complex reality of the moment.

And so we construct another syllogism: if music exhibits the quality of mutual penetration, and if the world *is* musical, then we have ground for thinking that the world as a whole exhibits this ghostly pattern of mutual habitation. Music's form is a trace of the form of the whole cosmos. And, we might be forgiven another hope: if what is, is music, perhaps there is a musician; and if the music manifests the enfolded melodies and rhythms of the world itself, then perhaps that musician does too. Maybe we can even speculate that the musician *is* the melody we overhear in the music of the spheres, the rhythm that strikes out the count of the cosmos.

As the ancients perceived, the musical qualities of the cosmos are replicated in human life. We pass on the vibrations of our excitement to others, so that our excitement evokes excitement. We pour our excited souls out to others, so that our enthusiasms dwell in them.

This is why thinkers like Jonathan Edwards often point to singing to portray an ideal society. According to Edwards, the heavenly city of the new Jerusalem is a company of people singing sweetly together. This isn't a theologian's fancy, but a real-life physical phenomenon. Singing a single text to the same music not only portrays community but actually creates it. You may have had the experience of singing with a large group of people. As you sing, the vibrations from the person next to you affect your body. Your bodies remain distinct, of course, but you are vibrating one another with a combined voice. Your voice inhabits the bass or tenor next to you, and that singer's voice sings through your body. The song unites the singers because it is the same song in and from each, but the singers are also united to each other as the vibrations of one body vibrate its neighbors.

Theologian Stephen Guthrie notes, "As we sing together we attend to the activity of our own bodies in making sound, and we regard and respond to our own song as we hear it resonate in the space around us. We hear and attune ourselves to the sound of others' voices. We respond not only to people, but to the physical qualities of sound we are creating with others and the physical and acoustical properties of the space in which we sing."[13] Roger Scruton makes a similar observation: "The coordination of movement in dancing and marching grants a vision of social order. But the movements here combined are seen as apart from one another, each occupying its exclusive space and expressing its distinctive goal. In music, however, all distance between movements is abolished, as we confront a single process in which multiplicity is simultaneously preserved and overridden. No musical event excludes any other, but all coexist in a placeless self-presentation. . . . It is as though these many currents flowed together in a single life, at one with itself."[14]

When we sing together, each voice provides the setting for every other; each is the room in which every other dwells, even as each dwells in the room provided by all the others. The sopranos provide a house in which the basses dwell, and the basses lay a foundation for an aural space within which other voices live, move, and have their being. The sounds of the whole choir penetrate each singer, even as the singers inhabit the sound they produce. Voices resound and circle back, so that the sounds that go out turn back to fill the singers' souls. Music is a Möbius strip, where inside and outside exist on a continuum, and music making is the form of mutually indwelling society, all sweetly singing together.

My theme has been an obsessive one. But at least it has the virtue of being singable. It is a *musical* theme.

7

Making Room

I have been describing what is, how the world is. We've climbed up from one level to another, pausing here and there, like Dante with Virgil, to look around and to figure out where we've come from and where we might be heading. So far, I've been engaged in an exercise in ontology. I've analyzed the relationship between human beings and their environments, objects, and tools; explored human relationships, especially erotic relationships expressed sexually; attempted to penetrate the mystery of time. We've talked of poetry, of metaphor and metonyms, of texts and intertexts and how language is capable of meaning anything at all; we've listened to some music.

Everywhere, at every terrace along the way, we've found that the landscape has familiar features: Things are irreducibly different. Things cannot exist at all unless they are distinct from other things. At the same time, these irreducibly different things mysteriously inhabit one another, pass into and out of one another, penetrate even as they are penetrated, envelop the very same things that envelop them. And we have found that, while things cannot be at all without being irreducibly distinct, they *also* cannot be at all without this mutual penetration. I can't exist unless the world I inhabit comes to dwell within me. I cannot have relationships with another person, most especially those whom I love, unless we pass into one another. Time exists only because past and present and future ineffably and simultaneously take up residence in each other. Words don't mean unless they occupy other words and are open enough to be occupied. Each note of music is different, but each note is what it is because other sounds resound through the sound it makes.

All this is, as I say, ontology. It's the way things *are*. We've thought a little about thinking—the problems of human knowing. We've done some epistemology, in other words, but we've done it under the heading of ontology, on the supposition that human knowing is another of the things that *are*, another of the complex realities of creation. We've pushed toward theology once or twice, because if this is the way things are we can't help but ask *why* they are the way they are. We can't help but ask the ontological question: Why is there *anything at all*? And we can't help but ask something more specific: Why are things *like this*? We're humans. We question. We're humans, so we want, even demand, explanations.

What we *haven't* done is ask what all this means in practice. Suppose you've embraced my theme as your own. Suppose you're convinced the landscape around us is just as I've described. But you still want to know, How then shall I live? What does it mean for me to live in *this* kind of world? Being human, you can't help but ask that question, and can't help but want an answer: What does all this mean for ethics?

Before we get to ethics, let's stay "meta" for a bit longer: What does it mean to live ethically? Are we ethical when we conform to nature? Are we being ethical when we regard the absolute demands of the moral law as the word of God? Are we being ethical when we obey the commands of the Torah or the Sermon on the Mount or the Qur'an or the Book of Mormon? when we submit to the guidance of a sage or guru? when we adjust ourselves to situations as they present themselves? Is the ethical life mainly about rules? about our dispositions? about dancing in step with our changing circumstances?

Does ethics somehow involve all this at once?

Something like the last suggestion is the best: ethics cannot be reduced to rules, dispositions, or situations without distorting ethics.[1] We apply rules differently from situation to situation, and we don't really know how a rule works or which rule to use unless we know the variations. You don't even know *which* rule to use unless you have examined the facts. "Love your enemies," Jesus said. To apply that, we need to identify our enemies. "Love your neighbor as yourself," Jesus said, quoting Leviticus. And the lawyer's response was a reasonable one: "Who *is* my neighbor?" "Don't covet your neighbor's wife or his house or his cattle," Yahweh thundered from Sinai, but you need to see a marriage certificate and a bill of sale to know what woman, house, and cattle are off-limits. You can't even use a rule unless you know something about the situation, since rules always have to be applied to a real world that is always in the form of a particular situation.

Rules cannot be followed without attention to situations, and the effort to sidestep situations is ultimately unethical. It's another version of the attempt to escape time and change that we've seen before.

On the other hand, you can't abandon rules and reduce ethics to situations either. Situational ethics is incoherent:

Master: Always conform to the situation.

Disciple: Is that an absolute command?

Master: How 'bout those Seahawks?

Worse, a purely situational ethics is ultimately unethical. Are we faithful only when situations demand faithfulness, or is faithfulness a trans-situational virtue? Asked whether rape might be legitimate under certain circumstances, no one will seriously answer, "Yes, of course. There are times when rape is the ethical course." If anyone *does* say that, you can be morally certain he is a philosophy professor, that he lives a highly protected life in the academy, and that he would have a very different reaction if the rape victim were his daughter or his wife.

Right dispositions are just as necessary. Doing the right thing for the wrong reasons is wrong because goals and motives determine what kind of action an action is. Taking care of an old lady out of greed for her inheritance is not an act of kindness, or even an act of kindness with a patina of disquieting immorality. It's a different sort of act entirely, an act of avarice. Conforming to the prescriptions of a religious ritual without real devotion to God is not worship but hypocrisy, a vice condemned by ancient Jews like Isaiah and Jesus, by Christians like Aquinas and Calvin, by the Buddha, Muhammad, and Hindu sages through the ages. Evil dispositions make an act evil, but good dispositions don't by themselves make an act ethical. We might pity the whore with the heart of gold, but the category of "well-meaning rapist" doesn't make any ethical sense.

So, the only way to be ethical or think ethically about ethics is to juggle all of these factors, to keep all the balls in the air all the time. And here we glimpse again the pattern we've encountered throughout this essay, the pattern of mutual indwelling, operating at the level of theory: ethical concepts and ethical authorities have to indwell each other to be truly ethical. If we extract rules from the intricacies of situations and the motivating power of dispositions, the rules are useless. If we siphon off situations from rules and dispositions, we will find ourselves justifying horrors. If we reduce ethics to dispositions, we can defend any action, so long as one's heart is in the right place.

Each has to be defined by the other. Rules apply to situations, and we conform to rules only when our motives and goals are right. Situations need to be seen in the light of ethical rules, since rules are part of the situation we're in. We can make sense of our ethical dispositions only when they attend to rules and remain attentive to situations. These three are one, because each is a home for the others; each makes its home in each. Unless each dwells in each, we don't have ethics at all. Ethics is constituted by the mutual indwelling of rules, real-life situations, and virtuous dispositions. When we inquire into the "ontology" of ethics, in other words, we find at a conceptual level the same pattern we found when exploring the world outside our heads. We discover the contours of mutual habitation. Since we're talking ethics, though, the "is" becomes a "must": ethics is a study of dispositions, rules, and situations. Ethics also *must* be such, or it ceases to be ethical.

Something is missing from this analysis of ethics: love.[2] When we tease out the reality of love, we can see that it too manifests the very same rhythm of reciprocal penetration, now on a practical rather than theoretical plane.

We all have our own projects and interests, and we create a small, enclosed, protected fortress around them and ourselves. Our minds are preoccupied with our own dreams and plans. We organize our time to reach our goals. If you are in a position of authority, you bend others into your projects, make them dance to the tune you pipe. When they don't cooperate, they become obstacles to your dreams, and they might have to be eliminated—which means different things depending on whether you run a Burger King or run illicit drugs.

Not surprisingly, the self-enclosed person is hostile to interruption, to the demands and claims of others. We meet "what is not part of the self-generated (and self-generating) project with refusal or a sense of defeat."[3] If I can't turn another person to my own purposes, that person is a roadblock, something to be run over and plowed under.

My employer gives me a project to work on, which eats up my free time and interferes with my plans. My teacher gives me an extra set of math problems, which means I can't watch the ball game or play on the Xbox. If you're an employer, the shoe is on the other foot: a recalcitrant employee stands in the way of realizing your goals for your company. A troublesome violinist keeps the conductor from achieving the artistic heights the conductor aspires to for the orchestra. A disabled or rebellious child pricks the bubble of the ideal of peaceful family life I had hoped for and expected.

The Christian existentialist Gabriel Marcel argued that instead of considering others as inconveniences, we should welcome them with expectant "availability." Availability is "the aptitude to give oneself to anything which offers, and to bind oneself by the gift. . . . It means to transform mere circumstances into 'opportunities,' we might even say favours, thus participating in the shaping of our own destiny and marking it with our seal."[4] Availability means accepting unexpected situations not only as gifts for me but also as opportunities to imprint myself on the other who intrudes. Mutual marking and dwelling-together is the result, but only if one is "available," only if one is willing to make room and take up room.

That problem employee might have something to offer and might be a potential recipient of some good I can give. That violinist might provide a fresh insight into a passage of the symphony. A disabled child doesn't destroy my dream of a loving family but challenges me to love in ways I never dreamed possible. When we are available, the other is no longer a wall or an invading army but a home, "a place where 'I' can dwell, at the intersection of receptivity and self-donation."[5]

The double character of this dwelling is important: the other is not only a potential recipient of my largesse but also a potential benefactor to me. As I consider him a place where I might dwell, I simultaneously offer my life as a place where he might dwell. Marcel highlights this doubleness with the ambiguous term "appeal." On the one hand, an "appeal" is a request, a petition for aid; on the other, it refers to attraction, the appeal of a handsome man, of a rose with morning dew, or of a cold drink on a hot day. For Marcel, "appeal" means both petition and attraction, and the two senses overlap. The petitioner is not merely someone in need, but also someone who attracts my delight and admiration. Availability thus is "realized in admiration, the 'eruption' of the self wherein it goes out in an actively enthusiastic receptivity toward the other."[6] Our reception of the other into ourselves is not grudging or surly. A grudging reception is nonreception, a refusal of the other's appeal (petition) because it is a failure to recognize the other's appeal (attractiveness).

To be truly available, we must be ready to receive *and* give simultaneously. Availability is a readiness to commit or pledge oneself to the one who makes appeal. I open a space in myself, where the other can "lay a claim," thus completing the cycle of mutual indwelling that began with me seeing the other as a "place" where I can dwell. If I make myself a dwelling place for others, I give them "property rights" in me, even as I assume property rights in them. I am his; he is mine.

In a word, availability is love, and it is a love to others within one's immediate circle that opens out beyond the circle in "absolute availability."[7] Not only my chosen others like my wife or husband, not only the close but unchosen loved ones like parents and children—not only those, but also strangers on the street, the beggar on the sidewalk, the enraged customer on the phone, the demanding boss, the resistant employee, the recalcitrant violinist, all are enclosed in the circle of my availability. We are to "encounter unexpected and even seemingly inhospitable circumstances as not ultimately an intractable impediment to my flourishing, but to encounter these circumstances in hope and trust as a new 'dwelling place' for my person."[8] Each is a potential dwelling place, a home, for others. When someone comes to the door and knocks, the *polite* thing to do is to invite them in. The *ethical* thing to do is to make yourself available, to open your life as they open theirs.

Other people *do* take up residence in us, whether we welcome them or not. We are who we are because of the others who "inhabit us." And living in love means that we allow this habitation, open our doors to others, and seek to dwell in them. The reality of mutual indwelling in human relationships implies an *ethic* of mutual indwelling: we indwell one another; therefore we ought to indwell one another. Be what you are. Be like the father in the son, the wife who welcomes her indwelling husband. Be the past memory and future anticipation inhabiting the present. Be the word in the word in the world. Be the music that enters and surrounds, the song that joins a multitude of voices into one.

In part, this penetration is psychological. In the middle of a crisis—a health threat, a challenge in our marriage or with one of our kids, a major vocational change, the necessity to make a major decision—our minds are preoccupied with the situation and the other people who are part of that situation. Not infrequently, they inhabit our dreams. We can't shake them. They are with us all the time until the situation is resolved.

Painful as it may be, this psychological occupation of our souls by other people should not be shaken off. Our openness to their habitation in our minds, memories, imaginations is an act of love. We make ourselves, our very souls, available to them. We become vulnerable to their fears, which become our fears; their worries and anxieties become ours. We bear their burdens in the deepest part of our psyche. And thus, painfully, our souls are enlarged.

Parents know what I'm talking about. When children get to the early stages of adulthood, parents are preoccupied with the friends they are choosing, the choices they are making. Parents cannot isolate themselves from their children and live at peace while their children go through crises on their own. Because they love them, their children inhabit them. And they should, because that is what love means.

Beyond psychology, our lives are occupied by other people. No one else lives inside my body, but my skin isn't the boundary of my life. My life extends to the things I do, the places I go, the people I love, and the strangers I meet. These things outside indwell us, even as we indwell them. The scope of my life extends to encompass all of these, and if I live in love, then I make room for them all.

This is most obvious with those people who literally occupy the same space with me, my family or roommates. Sexual union is a physical act of mutual habitation, but all other aspects of marriage manifest the same reality. Husbands make room for their wives in their lives, their projects, their dreams, their labors. Wives do the same. That is, husbands and wives *ought* to make room. All too often they don't, especially men. Men become preoccupied with their tasks, withdraw into themselves or barricade the entrances to their man caves, and in general create spaces with stern "No women allowed" signs on the door. Men resent the time and energy a woman takes up. They resent the way a woman's concerns and worries occupy their consciousness. Many wives have occasion to echo Portia's pained lament to Brutus: "Dwell I but in the suburbs of your good pleasure?"[9] Spouses who fail to make themselves available to one another are headed for trouble. It's a story that every marriage counselor, pastor, and family court judge knows all too well. A man withdraws from his wife, becomes reclusive and silent. His wife is desperate and demands entry. The husband buys a deadbolt, maybe two, to lock the door of his soul as firmly as he can. The more demanding and shrill the wife gets, the more the husband labors to preserve a space of peace and quiet. The more he backs away, the shriller she gets. They stop occupying the same bed, then stop occupying the same room. Before long, they are contemplating living apart permanently. Women may withdraw from the intimacy of marriage to devote themselves to children, to a career, to community service, to the titillation of flirtation or adultery.

They refused to make room for one another, and so they make their own rooms. Before they quite know what they've done, their failure of love, a failure of availability and openness, finally bears the only fruit it can: lovelessness and loneliness, separation and divorce. They refused to make room and now have no home for one another.

Parenting too is, literally, making room. A happy newlywed couple shares a bed, a dinner table, lazy mornings sipping coffee and surfing the web, quiet evenings reading or watching a movie. Into this idyll comes a needy infant, thrust screaming into their space. Gone are the leisurely mornings. They rise several times during the night (at least Mom does) to tend to the child. *Someone* has to get up whenever the baby decides the night is over. Evenings are spent battling colic, restoring order to the house in time for things to be scattered again the next day, washing the dishes and doing the laundry, settling a writhing infant, trying to hear the movie over the cries of the child in the crib in the next room.

The child adds fresh complications to the schedule, inhabiting the time as well as the space that the parents once had to themselves. Mom will lose time at work, and when she goes back to work she'll have to make arrangements for a sitter. She might have to quit work, but even if she stays at home, she'll have to make room in her schedule for changing diapers, nursing, preparing the baby food. Dad may pick up the slack somewhere—cooking dinner, putting the baby to sleep so Mom can rest. Both Mom and Dad will have to live with more disorder than they have been used to.

And that's not to mention the room that parents have to make for a new child in their affections. Newlyweds have the luxury, if they want to make use of it, of focusing exclusively on one another. Parents do not. Moms have to enlarge themselves to make room for the infant among their loves. Few mothers have any problem doing this. Having made room in their own body for the baby for nine months predisposes them to make room for the baby after birth. The baby emerged from their own flesh, and they naturally love it as their own body. Dads might have a harder time. Dad used to get all the strokes and sweet whispers his wife had to offer, but now she bestows the same affection liberally on her newborn. He may resent it, especially if the infant ends up sleeping between him and his wife: "When do I get a snuggle?" he will demand, bitterly.

Then another comes along. Maybe another. In some families, still another unaccountably follows, and so on. Each time, everyone in the family is challenged by the presence of the new member. Each new child brings new demands, fresh adjustments to the schedule, reconfigurations of rooms and furniture and living space, expansion of affections. Each new addition creates conditions for trouble. What if Child Number 2 doesn't like having to compete with Number 3 for Mom's attention and affection? What if she feels closed out, as if Mom's room is full to capacity and there's no more space, nowhere to add a wing or expand the bedroom? Children feel neglected and demand more attention. Dad may feel that the kids get all the attention anyway. Unless everyone makes more room, someone gets crowded out; perhaps everyone gets crowded out in one way or another.

Now that arranged marriages are mostly a thing of the past, most of us who are married have chosen our husband or wife. No prince told her she had to marry him; his parents didn't urge a plain woman on him to heal a breach between two noble houses. Making room for someone we choose—usually someone we have fallen in love with, someone we *want* to spend our life with—is not easy, but it's by far easier than making room for the total stranger who popped out of Mom, bawling and needy. Even parents who have chosen to be parents don't know what they are going to get.[10] The infant that shows up is an utter stranger. He's naked and hungry; she's never heard of a toilet, and for several months she can communicate her desires and wants only through inarticulate cries. He may have Down syndrome; she may be born with muscular dystrophy. Whether parents are prepared or not, the infant takes up residence, occupies the home, and begins to take charge. It takes a particular act of loving availability for parents to receive little strangers, and to make them a place that we wish to occupy in turn.

All the "wills" should be "musts." Most parents have children because they want children. But many parents don't know the sorts of demands the child will make on them. They don't realize how radically vulnerable, how thoroughly available, they have to make themselves if they are going to be successful parents. Some parents fail. When their lives are turned inside out to make room, some refuse to adjust, try to live on as they were, and decide there is no more room in the inn.

Even the best parents often slip into old habits of self-closure. Think of the last time you were in the middle of an important piece of work and one of your children came to you for a hug. At that moment, the child was not part of your "project" and was probably treated accordingly. A child who has to force out space for himself in the lives and affections of his parents may become an attention-getting class clown, a juvenile delinquent, a ticking bomb of explosive resentment. Whatever the outcome, a child whose parents have never made room for her is not going to be a healthy child.

Families become dysfunctional when they refuse or fail to make room. If the members of a family don't make room for one another, but consider each other competitive obstacles to love and security and success, there is no family. Siblings who do not go beyond this minimum never live as genuine brothers and sisters. They never mutually share hopes, dreams, secrets, joys, games, blood, and spit. They are living against the grain of the universe, living contrary to the pattern of mutually inhabiting love evident in the world around them.

Each individual must make room; the family as a whole must make room for nonfamily if it is going to be healthy. A family that refuses contact with outsiders can appear "strong" and "close-knit," but the dysfunctions of such isolated families are well known. Unless a home becomes home to more than the family, unless it opens itself out through hospitality and enters into the lives of others, it is not a family but a pathological fortress.

In larger groups—in churches, neighborhoods, cities—individuals equally have to make room for one another. Anyone who has been a conscious member of a larger group for more than a few years knows that this is not an altogether pleasant experience, and can be wrenchingly painful. Many lives are slums, as full of anger, violence, and bitter brokenness, as littered with trash and broken bottles, with discarded needles and failed hopes, as the darkest of America's inner cities. We don't want to live there, and we sure don't want them to move in with us. However, closing them out is not an ethical option. We should occupy the lives that open up to us, even if those lives carry a stench of decay and death. We should open our lives to the human wrecks we encounter, lest we be like the priest and the Levite in Jesus's parable about the good Samaritan.

This widens out into a social and political ethic since the same pattern should replicate itself at every level of society. Neighborhoods cannot close themselves off from neighboring neighborhoods. When they do they run the risk of turning into tribal encampments, connected only by their mutual hostility. Whatever might have been the case in the past, today no nation can remain impervious to other nations. The German company Mercedes Benz employs 3,000 Alabamans at its plant near Tuscaloosa, the Korean Hyundai has 2,500, and Honda has 4,000.

Alabama has made room for German, Korean, and Japanese companies and products, and Germans, Koreans, and Japanese have done the same on their end. The xenophobic reaction of some Americans is a reaction at war with reality, and a failure of love. Making room for others is as much a demand in international trade as in the home.

Some philosophers, like Jacques Derrida, say that hospitality must be absolute. We are to welcome all, and welcome them as they are. That is not the sort of ethic I propose here. Rather, it is an ethic of hospitality that welcomes in order to change. We don't welcome the naked so they can be naked in our presence; we don't show hospitality to the hungry so they can watch us eat. We welcome the naked and hungry to change their circumstances. We make room for them so we can clothe and feed them.

So too with moral hunger and personal shame. We don't welcome addicts so they can continue in their addiction. We make room for them, and take up residence in their lives, in order to be agents of ethical transformation. We don't receive the prostitute to help her get more tricks. We open our lives to the prostitute so we can deliver her from her slavery—to the pimp, perhaps to drugs, to poverty, to a destructive life. Hospitality is not universal approval. It is universal welcome for the sake of renewal. We make room not to tolerate but to transform.

We've made some advances in our turn from ontology to ethics, more than we might have noticed. From this point in our climb, we can begin to see the peak and begin to have something more than suspicions about what's up there. The nature of the universe as I've described it encourages an ethic of self-giving love; if we are going to live in accord with the shape of things, we need to adopt a stance of availability, of openness to others and willingness to enter when others open to us. And that suggests a way to reason back from ethics to ontology. If the ethics of mutual penetration is an ethics of love, then the ontology of mutual indwelling is an ontology of love. The world is open to me and I to the world. Persons are capable of being open to other persons, and times to other times. Words make room for other words, and chords have room for all the clustered notes that contribute to their sound. At every terrace, it seems, even when we were only looking through a glass darkly or hoping for some insight into the way things are, we were glimpsing traces of love, love wired into the world, love as the operating system of creation. And as we look up to the peak, we might begin to see the outlines of a love that moves the sun and all the other stars.

8

The Supple Imagination

Some people think with protractors and T-squares. Every thought is constructed with sharp cuts, and thoughts are combined at right angles. Everything depends on *this* not being *that*, on keeping *that* and *this* from touching or slopping into each other. Clear thought depends on the sharpest and most inviolable distinctions and boundaries between things and ideas.

The instinct goes back a long way. It appears in Plato's metaphysics as the dividing line between the sensible and the intelligible, between the world we experience and the world that truly *is*, the world of forms and ideas. It reappears in modern epistemology in the clear and distinct ideas that Descartes wants to use as the building blocks of everything we can know, and in the line of separation he draws between his thinking self and the spatial world around him. It comes out in the Cartesian fascination with geometric shapes and the aspiration to produce a philosophy of everything that takes the form of a geometry text, moving from undeniable axioms through irrefutable proofs to the edge of the universe. It shows up in scientific treatises and in books on everything from theology to poetry to art that pretend to be scientific.

Buried deep down under this way of thinking is a pattern of life and thought even more ancient than Plato. In the ancient world, boundaries between sacred and profane, between the holy and the common, gave life its structure. Within the boundary of the sacred is an ordered world, a world ordered by law and presided over by friendly, or at least friendlier, gods. Outside is a world of chaos and danger, where the wild things are. The world has, after all, been forged from a chaos onto which some gods or a subgod has imposed a certain degree of order. Unless firm walls are in place, the world will melt back into the goop it came from. We have to be able to sort through the whole pile of what is, placing everything on the right side of the wall, into its little box. Otherwise, all is mishmash. Clear and immovable borders are a prophylactic against chaos. Clear and immovable mental distinctions are a protection against intellectual chaos.

Even if we discard the mythical and mystical support, it's easy to see the attraction of sharp and clear distinctions. After all, things *are* different from each other. And if we want to think accurately about the world, we should acknowledge those differences. We should think with the grain of things and not against the grain, lest we end up with a brain full of splinters. It's impossible to be rational at all unless we acknowledge a radical difference between true and false, impossible to be ethical if we don't have exclusive categories labeled "right" and "wrong." It is or it is not true that human beings evolved from lower forms of life, and our opinions and instincts about a wide range of things depend on our answer to that question. Homosexual acts are either perfectly legitimate expressions of human love, or they are, as traditional Christian, Jewish, and Muslim teaching has said, unnatural and abominable, an abuse of human sexuality.

Whichever side of those debates we fall on, we are making all-or-nothing judgments. No matter how complex our answers to those questions may be, we are saying yes or no not only in the end but all along the way as well. Some things are real, some illusion. Some statements are false, some true. Some acts are moral, others immoral. Irreducible difference is one of the features of the world we inhabit. It's an essential part of our mental equipment. Relationships depend on the prior reality of difference. Without difference, there could not be any networks or patterns of relations among things. There's no difference in a blob.

Drawing lines and making distinctions is, however, only the beginning of engagement with reality. In many cases, a crisp division of the world into *this* and *that* doesn't work. That is, it doesn't match the way the world is. Is it raining or isn't it? It seems a simple question until you notice that the actual meteorological conditions involve a heavy mist, which is something between rain and not-rain.[1] How much moisture in the air makes it "raining" rather than "very, very foggy"? Any definite answer to this (so many water molecules per cubic inch) will be arbitrary. The fact is, rain and not-rain are at the ends of a continuum, and there are intermediate states between them. Members of my family have had long-standing debates about whether our various family vans have been blue or green, and it's a real debate because the color is somewhere on the spectrum between the two. And as long as we're talking about boundary-blurring phenomena, I have one final word: platypus.

Once the irreducibles have been recognized, we need to examine the often intimate, inseparable ways they join with one another. Once we notice a difference between inside and outside, we should also recognize the exchanges that constantly take place between them. Once we see that fathers and sons are different from each other, we should begin to notice the ways fathers live on in their sons and the way sons inhabit their fathers. More, we have to reckon with the fact that each side of each pair is *necessary* to the other. There is no outside without an inside, nor a father without a son. The objects and patterns of the world are co-defined by one another. They are what they are in reciprocal relationship. They exhibit something like the shape of love, and we can understand them only if our minds follow those contours.

Things leave traces behind even when they are absent. Language exhibits this quality everywhere. Words have unique sensible features and unique meanings, but they mean what they mean in part because of their differences from other words. If the word "pin" didn't exist in English then the word "pen" would have a different quality. The tiny difference of spelling and the tinier (sometimes nonexistent) difference of pronunciation bring the two words together constantly. When I say, "Reach me that pen," you might say, "I don't see a pin." "No," I say, irritably, "not *pin, pen*." When I said "pen," "not-*pin*" is part of what I meant. A vanishing trace of "pin" is present even in its absence.[2]

Words leave traces of themselves even in their opposites. "White" means, among other things, "not-black," but once we define white as "not-black," then white's opposite leaves its trace in the definition of white. Up is "not-down," and down is "not-up." Earth is not-sky, sky not-earth. Man and woman are "opposite" sexes but, much to the dismay of radical feminists, in English, the one leaves its trace in the other. "Man" is sitting there grinning at you from the word "woman" as the male is present in the "female."[3]

I enter the room where I slept as a child and memories flood back, memories I could not have conjured without the room to help. I remember conversations, games, fears, anxieties, dreams that I have not thought about for years. As I fell asleep in my childhood, the headboard of my bed became the control panel of a spaceship, the posts levers and the board covered with imaginary knobs and toggle switches. As I move through the house, the interaction of me and the house calls other incidents to memory. The sofa in my father's study still reminds me of my mother, who used to sit in one corner. The dining room table is not just any table, but in its setting and with its particular form it bears the traces of several dozen Thanksgivings and Christmas meals.

These things exist for other people too, and the memories they attach to the same objects are different. Other members of the family wouldn't experience the house or growing up in just the same way. But their experience would also be an experience in which traces of absent events play a prominent role. Their experience of the world is their interaction with the world, a product of their indwelling and the world's indwelling of them. They would find traces of the past in the present.

"Presence" and "absence" themselves display the same qualities. They seem to be opposites, but these opposites often leave traces in each other. I've heard that husbands are sometimes physically present but personally distant from their wives. (My wife, of course, has no such grounds of complaint about me, but I understand that other wives have reason to grumble.) Before we can answer the question, Is Jim present? we have to specify the kind of presence we're talking about. We might think that distinguishing between personal and physical presence would do the trick: He's *physically* present, but his *mind* is drifting elsewhere. It's actually more complicated than that. His mental or personal absence would not be an issue at all if he were not physically present. If he were off on a fishing trip, his wife would *expect* him to be mentally absent. In the sense we are using the terms, his personal absence *requires* his physical presence. A certain kind of absence is only possible if it is combined with a certain kind of presence. This kind of absence is impossible except as a disappearing trace of presence.

We are frequently met with these "aporias," these undecidable puzzles, this oscillation from one thing to its opposite and back, as we examine the contours of the world. One of the most important for Jacques Derrida, the father of deconstruction, was the aporia of origin. There can't be, he pointed out, any *pure* origin, an origin that is *only* origin without something added. An origin has to be supplemented if it is to be an origin at all. A spring that doesn't produce a flow of water isn't really a spring; a founding event that isn't followed by a succession of events originated nothing. Some years ago, I saw a website that boldly announced that it would be the center of future theological discussion. There was one lonely post on the blog, and then the site went silent. The announcement was not an origin because it wasn't followed by any supplements. Source and supplement are different and in some contexts come close to being opposites. But they require one another. We know that there's no supplement without a source, but we're less used to seeing that the opposite is true: the source needs the supplement too.

Contexts provide parameters for meaning, for language and for things and for people. "Green" describes the color of my lawn, is slang for "money" (for old-fashioned gangsters), and is short for "greenhorn," an inexperienced beginner. A soup tureen can be a beloved heirloom, an embarrassing wedding gift, or an impulse purchase from a visit to Target.

But contexts are not fixed and rigid. Contexts are elastic. Contexts have contexts. You can understand your life story on its own, in the context of the history of your family, in the context of the history of your country, in the context of the history of the world, in the context of the history of God's kingdom, or in the history of Darwinian evolution. None of these is the "right" context. The frame of reference depends on what you want to examine and how far you wish to discover links between distantly related things and events. In the context of the solar system as a whole, it's accurate to say that the planets revolve around the sun and the earth rotates. But when I look at the sky, I see the sun come up, rise through the eastern sky, reach a peak, and then descend through the western sky. It's *true* to say that the sun rises and sets.

Contexts can also be inverted. You might tell your life story in the context of your family history. But you could turn that around and make the history of your family an episode of your life story. Biographers do this on the assumption that their subject's family history is only interesting to readers because it is the history that led to the life of the famous person who is the biographer's person of interest. You can tell the history of a particular nation in the context of the history of the world, or, if you're an American, you can tell the history of the world as a prelude to the birth of the United States. My desk is set in the context of the library, but you could change the position of the camera and make the desk the context for the library, treating the library as something that exists for the sake of the desk. You can read the *Divine Comedy* in the context of Dante's *Vita Nuova* or the *Convivio*, or you can read the *Convivio* in the light of the *Comedy*. Because the *Comedy* is the better-known and more influential text, most take the latter option, but there's no reason why you can't do the first. Reading the *Convivio* as the "master text" and the *Comedy* as the secondary text might highlight certain features of the *Comedy* that you've missed. You can even read the *Comedy* in the context of later texts, texts that were inspired by or responded to Dante's. You can view the supplement in the context of the source, or the source in the context of the supplement.

A skeptic might say that the library is the context for the desk because it is the larger, more basic context. You can have a library without a desk. But a bigger context isn't necessarily more fundamental. Jesus occupied only one house in the town of Nazareth, but the town is important mainly because it is the town of Jesus. You can think about Jesus as a child of Nazareth, but it's obvious that Jesus also sets the context within which the town has to be understood. If I were ever to become a rock star, the fact that I sat at *this* desk in the library would make it the most important feature of the whole library. It might even become a shrine, a site of pilgrimage famed for its healing properties.

Inside and outside are divided by a clear boundary. There's a wall, with some windows and, fortunately, an air conditioner, between the hot Alabama sun and me. I'm inside the house, and what's on the other side of the wall is outside. But the inside and outside define each other. A single wall doesn't create an inside because it doesn't form an outside. There isn't an inside without a set of walls that creates an outside. It's true enough to say that "inside" and "outside" are opposites, but then we also observe that they are mutually defining. We have an external layer of skin that is our outside and a skeleton, muscles, circulatory system, and organs on the inside. As we saw in chapter 1, the boundary is permeable and porous, but my point here is different. Here the point is that two realities that seem to be polar opposites—inside and outside—are not really so, or not entirely so. They form a necessary pair, each defining the other. Neither makes sense, neither is what it is, without the other.

Concepts leave traces in other concepts. Words leave traces in their opposites. The me inside and the world outside fold in on each other. Parents imprint themselves on children, and the effect goes in the opposite direction as well. We can perform intellectual inversions imaginatively when our minds are trained nimbly to follow the folds of the real world.

This pattern of thought implies a certain style of argumentation. Arguments are forms of battle. We use battle metaphors to describe arguments: one argument defeats another; we make "points" in our arguments, and these points are intended to be "sharp" and "penetrate the armor" of our opponent; we represent arguments as "battles of ideas" that provoke some of the same passion as physical battles. Your ideas are battering rams that you hope will break out chunks of your opponent's defensive walls until eventually the wall comes atumblin' down.

All these metaphors of argument assume that the opponents are set off from each other by a clear, straight, impenetrable boundary. You are in your trench and your opponent is in his, with a dangerous no-man's-land between. If you assume that and want to mount an argument, you've got to shoot at the fortress until it breaks.

If the world is folded, curved on itself, bent and swiveled and swirled and whirled and turned in on itself by mutual enfolding, if we think that things and concepts contain traces of their opposites, if we conclude that the pattern of the world is a pattern of music, language, and love, then we can begin to imagine a set of more subtle strategies for argument. Instead of lining up our hoplites in a dense formation and moving relentlessly forward until we meet the enemy, we look for our opponent's weak spot so that we can use it to flip him upside down. Argument isn't trench warfare but jujitsu. We need not be Achilles in argument; we can imitate Odysseus, that sly man of many devices.

Take this, for instance: Today's polarized and highly combative political debates often turn on the role of the state in social and economic life. On the one side are "liberals" who think the state has a positive role to play in economic and cultural life, evening out the inequities of market competition and supporting the marginal or oppressed who wouldn't have a chance to succeed without assistance. On the other side are "conservatives" or "libertarians" who believe the state has a very limited or no role to play in economic life, other than to punish fraud and other criminal acts, and to provide for the common defense in such a way that economic actors can go about their business without fear of invasion or insurrection or criminal attack.[4]

Debates are premised on the distinction between "state" and "economy." Both sides argue as if they agree that these are in reality distinguishable entities, such that one can influence the other duly or unduly. The difference is that one thinks that the entity of the "state" should influence the entity called the "economy," and the other doesn't.

In the real world, "economy" and "state" indwell one another. There is no economic activity without some form of legal or customary order.[5] All our economic activity takes place in a legal framework that interferes with the most basic features of economic life. Many of our economic transactions are governed by explicit contracts. I signed a contract with Baker Publishing Group to write this book, and both Baker and I are ruled by the terms of our agreement. If either the publisher or I default on the contract, the other would have legal recourse. As soon as contracts are signed, the legal system is invoked as the ultimate backup to enforce the performance of economic acts. Even when there is no explicit contract, our economic transactions usually operate with some form of implicit contract. I purchase a soup tureen from Walmart's vast selection of soup tureens, and if I find it damaged, I can return it for a refund or another tureen. If Walmart refuses to provide me with an unbroken tureen, I have recourse to the complaints department and might be able to pursue it further.

The "economy" is not separate from the "political" system. Laws are embedded in our economic activity. Politics is not on the outer boundary of the economy, policing the borderland. Politics indwells the economy. And vice versa. Lobbyists, voters, politicians—every politically active person is an economic actor. At the corrupt extreme, they make political decisions based on economic incentives. That powerful politicians pass laws to benefit themselves and their close friends and families is not fantasy; lobbyists and other hangers-on manipulate the system to the advantage of themselves and their friends. *Mr. Smith Goes to Washington* is fiction; *Mr. Abramoff Goes to Washington* isn't. Even the purest politician is an economic actor.

Military contractors make a lot of money, and a politician who is able to attract a defense contractor into her district is creating jobs. Members of Congress and governors (no matter whether they're liberal or conservative) give tax and other incentives to large companies to entice them to set up shop in their state. That aids the economy of the district and wins political points for the politician. Everyone goes home happy (except for businesspersons who can't afford a lobbyist or are too politically inept to get on the gravy train). To say this is "political" rather than "economic" activity is absurd. Everyone goes home happy precisely because politics and economies are cozy bedfellows.

Americans enjoy celebrating the lone inventor and the self-moving entrepreneur. Yet many of the most innovative technological breakthroughs of the past several decades began as government projects. The military invented the internet; the US government, not Steve Jobs, initiated research on smartphones. Even without that kind of direct aid, every entrepreneur and inventor in American history has benefited from the stability, freedom, and wealth that the American government helps to provide. Obama was right: no economic achievement was solely the work of one person or even a handful. Entrepreneurs are impressive humans, but they rely, as does everyone, on common goods that the "state" provides. It's not an accident that there are few entrepreneurs and inventors coming out of Afghanistan or Sudan these days.

Once we see that political actions and economic actions are not cleanly separated, we understand better the usual inconclusive clashes that take place every day on talk radio, Fox News, and MSNBC. There never is a choice between "state involvement in economics" versus "no state involvement." The two are abstractions, and in reality each is deeply embedded in the other. The supple imagination will recognize this, and make its moves accordingly. We can look for slippery ways to get past the stalemates.

Take this, for example: "Liberals" are supposed to look out for the interests of common people, while "conservatives" have a reputation for defending moneyed business interests. The best conservative arguments, however, are not the ones that defend big business. That builds a fan and donor base and solidifies the walls that liberals are trying to penetrate. It's also a good way of enhancing power. But it's *not* a good way of advancing constructive public debate. The best conservative arguments don't minimize the interests of poor Americans, but rather highlight them. The best conservative arguments make the case that conservative policies actually do more good for the people liberals claim to defend than liberal policies do.[6] Religious "social conservatives" are at their best when they argue that defending traditional sexual morality and "family values" benefits the poor and makes it more likely that the poor can rise above poverty. The most convincing antiabortion arguments are those that argue for restrictions on abortion because of our responsibility to protect the vulnerable, and they are convincing because they use rhetoric that is more common among abortion's defenders.

Liberal arguments could, in turn, stress the central aims of conservatives and turn them upside down. It might go like this: "Yes, one of the government's primary roles is defense, and *for that very reason* America should abandon its foreign policy adventuring, because that leaves our country more exposed to terrorists."

In my own field of theology, many operate with flat-edged systems that they use as blunt instruments for bludgeoning people who disagree. Theological systems become heavily defended fortresses to keep the undesirables at a distance. The supple imagination looks for alternative ways to upend opponents.

Suppose, for instance, a "charismatic" Christian is debating a "noncharismatic" Christian about the Holy Spirit. Charismatics are Christians who believe that the miraculous gifts of the

Spirit continue in the present. Just like the apostles, Christians today speak in other tongues, prophesy, and see visions. Many other Christians believe that these gifts were unique to the first Christians, miraculous confirmations of the good news when it was first new, and are no longer operative.

The noncharismatic might—he often does—attack the charismatic for making too much of the Spirit. "What about the Father and Jesus?" he demands, somewhat imperiously. "You're drunk with the Spirit and have neglected the weightier things." With the flat edge of his system he tries to pound some sense into the charismatic.

There's a more excellent way. Instead of arguing that the charismatic makes too much of the Spirit, the noncharismatic could begin by agreeing: "Yes, noncharismatics have made too little of the Spirit." Then comes the jujitsu: "And your charismatic understanding of the Spirit's work is far too limited. After all, the Spirit is with us, guiding and goading us, not only in the spectacular events of life, not only in the overwhelming experiences of prophecy or vision. The Spirit of Jesus is with us all the time, and that means all sorts of experiences and actions are guided and empowered by the Spirit. The young people who visit Alzheimer's patients in the nursing home are being driven into that ministry by the Spirit. The Wycliffe translator in Côte d'Ivoire is exercising the Spirit's gift of tongues just as much as the prophet who stands up at a prayer meeting to announce the word of the Lord. The administrative pastor who makes sure that things run smoothly is keeping in step with the Spirit who is the Spirit of order, not confusion. The fact that the translator has been trained, that her translations emerge after years of study, doesn't make her work any less miraculous, any less a work of the Spirit." By focusing on the spectacular, the charismatic hasn't made too much of the Spirit but too little.

Another example: Theologians have long puzzled over questions of free will. If God knows all things, including the future, then all things, including the future, are determined ahead of time. God won't be surprised, and if he can't be surprised, then nothing is going to happen other than what he expected to happen. The difficulties become acute for Christians who believe, as I do, that God not only knows but controls all things.

How then can human beings have any freedom or be held responsible for their actions? Theologians often answer this sort of question with a concession: *although* God knows all things that will happen in the future, still human beings are free. This assertion suggests that God's infallible knowledge and human freedom are incompatible with one another, and have to be stuck together in spite of being fundamentally at odds. Here and in many other cases, it is much better to begin that sentence with "because": *Because* God infallibly knows and controls the future, human beings are free and responsible. That seems to make things worse, and to sacrifice incompatibility to incoherence. But that move implies that God's knowledge and human freedom are not two doctrines awkwardly standing side by side, each waiting for the other to ask for the next dance. God's knowledge and human freedom depend on each other. Human freedom is embedded in God's infallible knowledge of the future, and God's infallible knowledge of the future somehow indwells human freedom.[7] Stating the issue with "because" implies that the two are always already dancing.

How can that be? That's a puzzle, but it's the *right* puzzle. It's a supple puzzle, a puzzle that brings illumination rather than stalemate. And there is sense to it: if God could be surprised, that would mean that the world is outside of God's control, and something other than God is directing events. If things are outside God's control, they're outside of *everyone's* control, because God is by definition the one who is most in control. (Alternatively, one could say that some other being or force is more in control than God is. That's a common viewpoint, but not one compatible with Christian theology.) If the universe is out of control, if it is chaotic, then there is no meaningful human freedom at all. There is only randomness, and if there is only random chaos, then human beings cannot be held responsible for anything. No matter what they do, it is no more than a twitch in the fabric of things. To be held responsible, human beings have to have some sort of control over themselves and their actions. If the world were outside control, there could be no freedom, no responsible action.

Whether or not these arguments are altogether convincing, they serve to illustrate the style of argument and investigation that matches the way the world is. Distinctions need to be made. Lines need to be drawn. Truth is not error; bad is not good. But instead of sharp angles and straight edges, we should learn to think in folds, in curves and Möbius strips, because the supple imagination follows the folded, interwoven, intertwined contours of the world we live in.

As in ethics, so in rationality, logic, and rhetoric: we follow the grain of the universe as our thinking and speaking, our arguing and debating take account of the mutual penetration of concepts and things. In fact, we cannot be rational at all unless our thinking gropes its way along these pathways. This is true in part because it is irrational to deny reality, and reality is a pattern of mutual indwelling. It is also true because our every thought and argument depend on the mutual penetrating of our minds and the world, of other persons and ourselves, of time and language. We cannot think without being, and we *are* only as indwelled and indwelling beings. We can't argue at all without language, and language is a system of significant signs, a mutual penetration of sense and intellect. We cannot persuade without words whose meanings come from the past into the present, without passion that urges our listeners to begin realizing the future now. Mutual indwelling is not an adornment for rationality. It is its essence, and we are "rational creatures" only because we and the world are as we and the world are.

9

I in Thee, Thou in Me

Throughout this book, I have been calling attention to a pattern that I claim is a deep structure of the real world, of human life, and of experience. The world is *not* patterned by mutually opposing things, concepts, or qualities that need to be kept in "balance." Things are much more intricately interlaced. The world is designed according to a pattern I've called "mutual indwelling," "reciprocal habitation," "interpenetration." I've used words like "intertwining" and "interleaving" and "twists" and "swirls, whirls, curves, and curls." I've written of how things circle back on themselves, of Möbius strips and Celtic knots. I claim to see this pattern everywhere—in physical reality, in language, sound, sex, personal relations, ethics, and the concepts we form to understand the world. I've tried to convince you that it's out there too.

My confrontation with the world takes this shape. I am not the world and the world is not me, but neither I nor the world exists independently of the other. I'm in the world, moving, acting, changing, and I can be in the world only if edible, drinkable, breathable bits of the world come into me. I learn things when the outside comes in, when I see and hear and smell and touch, when I learn from teachers and traditions and books.

That form of indwelling is largely physical, but sometimes the interpenetration of me and the world is more subtle, more conceptual. My hammer and my computer don't depend on me for their existence, but they are *defined* by the ways I use them. My computer is not just an object, objectively separate from me. I define what it is, a computing device, when I sit down to type or surf the web or answer email. I penetrate the very essence of the thing called "*my* computer." It would not be what it is if it were someone else's, or if it were incapable of computing. Things are in things too, again in a conceptual sense, since the objects in the world help to define one another, the cup defined by the coffee that fills it, a window by the wall into which it's inserted.

My confrontation with the world of other persons has a similar shape. I started life literally dwelling in another human being, and that other human being penetrated me too—Mom's food and drink and air and nutrients and blood were mine. Even after I separated from Mom, I still occupied her life, and she mine. My identity, my emotional instincts, my verbal and physical habits, my deepest desires, all were stirred up from outside. The things that make me *me* didn't come from me. I am what I am because others have poured themselves into me, so as to live in me.

My encounter with my wife exhibits the same intertwining in a more intense form. In sexual union, two persons, of opposite sex, become one flesh, mutually penetrating and enclosing. And that sexual union is a sign of a life lived together, as an intertwined thread of narrative, one complex fugue. The mutual indwelling of our lives didn't just change each of us; it changed the whole world for each. I dwelling in my wife, and my wife in me, means that we together inhabit the world as mutually indwelling partners.

Time exhibits this form. Past, present, and future are distinct, and yet there is no experienced time except as they fold back on each other. Past events reverberate in the present; objects made in the past occupy my world now. Future expectations and commitments determine what I do today. I would not experience time at all if this interfolding were to cease, if I were left with only a succession of disconnected present moments. I wouldn't even be able to recognize change if I didn't have some memory of what was, so as to compare it to what is; and some memories, good and bad, insistently impinge on my present life.

Language is a complex interknotting of word and world. Language is a human tool for understanding and acting in the world, and as soon as we speak or write, we translate the world into words. Saying "swan" brings the white feathered and winged thing into language. Words exist only because sense penetrates sound and sign, and because sign and sound make their home in meaningful ideas. Sequences of words only make sense because each word makes room for the word that follows, and because the words spoken in the past continue to dwell in the present. Literary texts are what they are by the indwelling of other literary texts in quotation, allusion, and echo.

Sound and music are perhaps the clearest illustration of the pattern I'm describing. Sounds exist quite literally within other sounds. A single note on the piano is "indwelled" by its overtones, and at the same time sounds through those overtones. In a chord, each sound provides a setting for every other, and in a melody line each note, like a word of a poem, falls silent to make room for the next. When we sing, we form a community of sound, each voice singing the same song, soprano setting the context for bass even as bass frames soprano. When we sing, each singer sings through others, literally vibrating the flesh of the singer's nearest neighbors. Music is perhaps our most elaborate, and most lovely, clue to the nature of the universe and our hopes for human society.

This is the way the world is, and because this is the way the world is, we should adopt a way of life that conforms to its pattern. Others indwell our lives; therefore we ought to open our lives hospitably to them. We indwell the lives of others; therefore, we ought to see others not as obstacles to our plots and projects but as potential homes in which we can dwell together. A world of mutual interpenetration implies an ethic of hospitality, welcome, invitation, companionship, centered on a common table.

And because this is the way the world is, we should learn to think nimbly along its curves and twists, its folds and coils and curls. Distinctions must be made, and without distinctions, rational thought, moral judgment, practical life become impossible. But things move back and forth across the boundaries we draw, and we should learn the supple art of argumentative judo. Instead of pummeling with a head-on attack, we should learn to use our opponents' weightiest arguments to knock them flat.

Throughout the book, I have made the strongest argument I could come up with regarding this pattern of mutual interpenetration. I have argued that this pattern is not only a somewhat helpful way to make sense of the world. I have argued, brashly, that the world *only* makes sense if we recognize this recurrent pattern. I don't exist in relation to the world unless the world penetrates me. I don't have any identity or character as a unique individual unless others dwell in me. Time is meaningless unless it houses past, present, and future simultaneously. Language exists only when sense penetrates sign and sign dwells in sense. Sounds are what they are because other sounds reverberate through them. I love only when I open myself to invasion and when I willingly invade others.

I have also contrasted this supple way of thinking to the very common habit of trying to "balance" opposite forces, concepts, objects, and so on. We "balance" only when there are two separable things to balance. Balance is the skill you need on a tightrope or when you're weighing out gold, but it's not the primary skill for understanding the world, because the world is not made up of separable items. We can "balance" one thing against another only if we have already wrenched apart things that belong together, when we have disentangled the tangles that make them what they are. We can "balance" individual and society only if we ignore the fact that they are mutually constituting; when we seek to balance past and present, we have to first tear asunder things that God has bound together.

That's a brash argument, but in this final chapter I'll make a brasher one. Not only do I claim to discern this pattern, but I also think I know where it comes from and why it is so pervasive in the world. To make my case, I have to turn to a more theological mode of discourse than I have used in the rest of the book.[1] As we've climbed from terrace to terrace, I've stopped to show you how things stand, and as we have ascended, I've suggested a few times that there is *something* at the peak that can explain the features of the landscape that has become more and more visible as we climb. As we've looked through a glass darkly, and suspected hopefully that we could see more, we have finally come to the conclusion that the world everywhere bears traces of love, and we've begun to suspect that that something at the peak has the same shape. In this final chapter, I will introduce you to that something. I want to introduce you to Love.

In theology, there is a venerable term that describes the kind of relationship I have been exploring throughout the book: "perichoresis." What I have been describing is the "perichoretic" shape of reality. Historically, the term has been applied to the relations of the divine and human natures of Christ, and the inner life of the Triune God. According to Christian orthodoxy, there is only one God, but this one God exists as three divine persons, Father, Son, and Holy Spirit. It's not that the one God is a shape-shifter who appears in different guises at different times. That notion, known as "modalism," was early on condemned as heresy. It's not as if the three persons make a binding commitment to do everything together, like the three musketeers. The doctrine of the Trinity is more mysterious and demanding than that. It states that the God who exists is one God precisely because he is the communion of the three, and he is the three precisely because he is the One God. Trinitarian theology doesn't abandon monotheism. It claims to be the truth of monotheism.

My purpose here and throughout the book is neither to explain nor to defend that basic orthodoxy, but rather to explore the one dimension of the reality of God that has been described with the term "perichoresis." Though never raised to creedal status, the term "perichoresis" goes back to the early church, has been used by many theologians through the centuries, and has become massively important to a number of contemporary theologians.[2] The word derives from a Greek verb (*perichōrein*) that means "to contain" or "to penetrate." First used to describe the unmixed union of divinity and humanity in Jesus, it has been more commonly used to describe the communion of the three persons of the Trinity as mutually "indwelling," "permeating," or "interpenetrating" one another. Each person within the Trinity is irreducibly himself. The Father is never Son, nor the Son Father, nor is either ever the Spirit. Yet these irreducibly distinct persons are united in an intimate fellowship of mutual indwelling. Within the Trinity, each person both wholly envelops yet is wholly enveloped by the others. Each person is both the dwelling place of and is indwelled by each of the others. The Father contains the Son, even as the Son contains the Father. The Spirit finds a home in the Son, while in the same movement the Son sets up house in the Spirit. As you've climbed through this book, you've discovered trace after trace of this pattern of mutual indwelling. What we've been finding all along the path, I submit, are traces of the Trinity.

Hilary of Poitiers expresses his astonishment at the mystery of God's perichoretic fellowship.

> It seems impossible that one object should be both within and without another, or that (since it is laid down that the Beings of whom we are treating, though They do not dwell apart, retain their separate existence and condition) these Beings can reciprocally contain One Another, so that One should permanently envelope, and also be permanently enveloped by, the Other, whom yet He envelopes. This is a problem which the wit of man will never solve, nor will human research ever find an analogy for this condition of Divine existence. But what man cannot understand, God can be.[3]

Perichoresis is a common inheritance of Latin and Greek churches. In the East, John of Damascus writes that the three persons

> dwell and are established firmly in one another. For they are inseparable and cannot part from one another, but keep to their separate courses within one another, without coalescing or mingling, but cleaving to each other. For the Son is in the Father and the Spirit: and the Spirit in the Father and the Son: and the Father in the Son and the Spirit, but there is no coalescence or commingling or confusion. And there is one and the same motion: for there is one impulse and one motion of the three subsistences, which is not to be observed in any created nature.[4]

The persons exhaustively indwell one another, containing and being contained, but at the same time, the differences between the persons remain absolute. The Father never becomes the Son, no matter how thoroughly he dwells in and is indwelt by him, nor the Son the Father.

John Donne's imagination was fired by the "slipperiness" and "entangling" of the perichoretically entwined persons.

> O Blessed glorious Trinity,
> Bones to Philosophy, but milke to faith,
> Which, as wise serpents, diversly
> Most slipperinesse, yet most entanglings hath,
> As you distinguish'd undistinct
> By power, love, knowledge bee,
> Give mee a such selfe different instinct
> Of these; let all mee elemented bee,
> Of power, to love, to know, you unnumbred three.[5]

All the traces of the Trinity that we've explored find their source and root in the fellowship of Father, Son, and Spirit, each of whom indwells each in a far more profound and exhaustive fashion than we find in creation. Because the Father is in the Son, we live in a world where I am in the world as the world is in me. The Father-Son-Spirit relation is the archetype of all human relationships, including sexual and romantic relationships. The Father is the source, and so linked with the past; the Spirit proceeds from the Father and Son, and so is the Spirit of the future; and the Son indwelled by the Source and Spirit is the "present" of the divine life. The Father is a speaker who indwells the eternal Word by the Breath that is the Spirit, and that Breath who is the Spirit is the music of God who lends melody and rhythm to the Father's Word. The Father, Son, and Spirit live in a harmony and love that is a model for human life: the Father makes room in himself for the Son, the Son for the Spirit, the Spirit for the Father and Son, and so the Trinity is the perfect and eternal communion reflected in dim and distant ways in families, churches, and peoples. The Trinity is the uncreated original of perichoretic rationality, for the Father knows himself in the Others, the Son and the Spirit, and the eternal Word understands himself as the One indwelled by the Father and Spirit.

None of the persons seeks his own; none seeks to know himself in isolation. Irreducibly different as they are, they are entangled in an eternal knot of perfect communion. Widespread as this notion is in trinitarian theology, it can seem a pointless exercise in mystery-mongering. As if confessing that the Christian God is both Three and One didn't put enough strain on rationality, Christians have to add that each of the three is indwelled by and indwells, contains and is contained by, each of the others. Why multiply the mystery? And if perichoresis is, as Hilary claims, a divine reality without created analogy, what difference can it possibly make anyway?

This entire book is a rejoinder to Hilary. I have argued that, far from being an exclusively divine reality, perichoresis is imprinted on creation and human life at every level, and that we only understand the shape of creation rightly when we recognize these traces of the Trinity. We live in a perichoretically shaped world.

That, I think, is the way Jesus speaks about perichoresis in the Gospel of John, which is the main biblical source for the concept. Jesus doesn't use the term, but he describes the reality that theologians later labeled as "perichoresis." And when he does, Jesus highlights the *similarities* between divine perichoresis, the church's relationship with him and the Father, and Christians' relations with one another. On behalf of his disciples, Jesus asks the Father "that they may all be one; even as Thou, Father, art in Me, and I in Thee, that they also may be in Us" (John 17:21). The Son is "in" the Father, and yet at the same time the Father is "in" the Son. Jesus prays that the unity of the disciples would be like—"even as"—the unity of the Father and Son, a unity already described as perichoretic. The mutual relations of the human persons who make up the church are to form an earthly image of the mutual relations of the persons of the triune fellowship. Jesus even prays that the disciples will be brought into the perichoretic fellowship of the Father and Son. Their unity with the Father and Son is also an "in/in" relationship. On the one hand, it is "them" (the disciples) in "Us" (the Father and Son); on the other hand, it is also "I" (Jesus) in "them" (the disciples), and "Thou" (Father) in "Me" (Jesus; John 17:23).

For John, perichoresis is not a sideshow. In fact, as John presents it, the gospel depends on the reality of divine perichoresis. The news is good only if the Father is in the Son and the Son in the Father.

John begins his Gospel by stating that "no one has seen God at any time" (John 1:18). This is a problem. For John, seeing is knowing (6:40; 11:45; 14:7), and knowing/seeing the Father and Son *is* eternal life (John 17:3). If the Father is hidden, we can find no way that leads to life. We need some way to behold him. For John, the good news is that there is such a way, and the name of that Way is Jesus.

When John speaks of the invisibility of God the Father, he is not primarily making a philosophical claim. God is invisible (see Col. 1:15–16; 1 Tim. 1:17), but John's main point has to do with the progress of salvation in history. His point is to stress that the Father has been invisible, until *now*, until the Word becomes flesh.

John first brings out a contrast of the old and new in 1:14. As everyone who has heard a sermon on John 1 knows, the word normally translated as "dwell" can be translated as "tabernacled" or "pitched a tent." The eternal Word moved into our neighborhood by taking human flesh, and in so doing he has shown the glory of God. But notice: when the glory came into the tabernacle in the Old Testament, everyone, including Moses and the priests, evacuated the tent (Exod. 40:34–38; 1 Kings 8:10–11). Now, the Word of glory descends in the flesh, and "we saw His glory" (John 1:14).

John describes the same contrast in different terms in 1:17–18. John's statement that "no one has seen God" refers back to the experience of Moses on Mount Sinai. When Moses asked to see

God, the Lord responded, "You cannot see My face, for no man can see Me and live" (Exod. 33:20). Moses was shown the "back" of God's passing glory, but not his face (Exod. 33:22–23). Now, though, having become flesh, the Word expounds the Father to us (John 1:18; see 2 Cor. 3). It is no longer true that "no one has seen God." On the contrary, Jesus says that those who have seen him have seen the Father (John 12:45; 14:9), and claims that his words and works display the Father's words and works (John 5:19; 12:49). In Jesus, the invisible God has become as visible, audible, tangible as any human being (see 1 John 1:1).

Jesus explains that his "exegesis" of the Father is rooted in his eternal relation to the Father. The issue that dominates the discussion at the beginning of John 14 is the "way." Jesus has said he is returning to the Father (13:33; 14:2), and tells the disciples they know "the way where I am going" (14:4). Jesus himself is "the way" to the Father (14:6) because the Father, the destination, is already and has always been "in" the way, that is, in the Son (14:7, 9–11). In Jesus, way and destination unite. Jesus can "show us the Father" (v. 9) because the Father is in him and he is in the Father. The good news that the Father has shown himself depends on the good news that the Father is in the Son. This is the perichoretic gospel.

What Jesus says about the "dwelling places" that he is preparing in his "Father's house" reinforces this point. Though often taken as a reference to heavenly cottages, the "Father's house" in John is the temple that is the body of Jesus (2:16–22), which is the "Father's house" in the sense that it is the place where the Father resides (14:10–11). The Son is the permanent and eternal "home" of the Father, as the Father is the eternal home of the Son. When the Son comes into the world, we get a glimpse of the "home life" of the Father with his Son. Through Jesus's tabernacling and ascent, the Father's house becomes a home for believers. Jesus goes away to prepare a place in his Father's house, in the temple of his body, for believers (14:2–3). The word for "dwelling places" is used elsewhere only in John 14:23, where it describes the *believer* as the place where Father and Son take up residence. Jesus is the dwelling of the Father, and becomes the dwelling place for believers. As a result, Jesus becomes the meeting place of the Father and his people. In him, in the house that is the Son, believers have family fellowship with the Father. Jesus is the common home for his Father and for his brothers.

This is the background for Jesus's prayer in John 17, where the mutual penetration of the Father and Son extends in an ecclesiological direction. Jesus offers a prayer for "those also who believe in Me through their word": "[I ask concerning] those . . . who believe in Me through their word; that they may all be one; even as Thou, Father, art in Me, and I in Thee, that they also may be in Us; that the world may believe that Thou didst send Me" (vv. 20–21). The text moves from the scattered hearers of the word, gathering them into a unity that reflects the perichoretic unity of the Father and Son and is rooted in the disciples' dwelling-in the Father and Son, a unity that manifests Jesus's identity and mission to the world. The unity of the church is modeled on the unity of the Father and Son ("just as"). Jesus prays that disciples will indwell one another in a way that dimly mimics the exhaustive eternal indwelling of the divine persons. More, the church is unified in this way because it has become a participant in the mutual indwelling of Father and Son. The church is not merely an *image* of the eternal dance of triune life, but is introduced to the dance as the bridal partner.

This perichoretic unity of the church, further, is integral to the church's mission. If the church is not a place where the members "dwell within" one another's lives, the world will not believe that the Son "dwells within" and "came forth from" the Father. For John, the good news is that the Father who has *not* been seen has *now* been seen in the Son, in whom the Father dwells. The Father who is not known has made himself known in Jesus. Beyond this, the Father has not only shown himself in the Son, in whom the Father lives, but has also brought us into the fellowship of Father and Son. The good news is that through the Son the Father has made room for us in *himself*, through his Son. Alternatively, the good news is that God has made *his* home in *humanity*, in the Word made flesh and in those who have become hearers and followers of the Word. Humanity was created for union with God, and in Christ the incarnate Son, God has joined himself with us, "I in them, and Thou in Me" (17:23).

Paul's is not a different gospel. For Paul too, the incarnation "works" because God himself is at work in the life, death, and resurrection of Jesus. "God in Christ" has forgiven sinners (Eph. 4:32), since "God was in Christ reconciling the world to Himself, not counting their trespasses against them" (2 Cor. 5:19).

As a result of this work of reconciliation, human beings are given a share in the perichoretic life of God. On the one hand, those who believe are "in Christ." In Christ, they are "alive to God" (Rom. 6:11), made alive in Christ the last Adam (1 Cor. 15:22; Eph. 2:6), so as to receive the gift of eternal life (Rom. 6:23). Those who are in Christ escape condemnation (Rom. 8:1–2) and are sanctified, made saints (1 Cor. 1:2), and brought near to the temple of God (Eph. 2:13). In Christ is liberty (Gal. 2:4) and justification (Gal. 2:17) and adoption as sons (Gal. 3:26). In the euphoric opening sentence of Ephesians, Paul announces that the Father of Jesus blesses us with "every spiritual blessing in the heavenly *places* in Christ" (Eph. 1:3), seated us in the heavenly places (Eph. 2:6) with and in Christ in whom all things are summed up (Eph. 1:10). The life of the disciple is "hidden with Christ in God" (Col. 3:3). Christ is the home for believers, and a richly adorned home he is.

But if Christ is home for believers, believers are equally a dwelling place for Christ. "I have been crucified with Christ," Paul says, and Christ now "lives in me" (Gal. 2:20). The mystery that Paul preaches among the gentiles is "Christ in you, the hope of glory" (Col. 1:27). Elsewhere, Paul says that the Spirit, not Christ, dwells in us (2 Cor. 1:22; cf. Rom. 5:5), and this forms the background for Paul's claims that believers are "temples" and dwelling places of God in the Spirit (1 Cor. 3:16; 6:19). Paul's very frequent address to believers as "saints" (*hagioi*) is shorthand for this temple theology: those in whom the Holy Spirit dwells are consecrated by the glory that is the Spirit, constituted as saints. At the same time that the Spirit is in believers, believers are "in the Spirit" (Rom. 8:9; Rev. 1:10; 4:2; 17:3; 21:10).

Believers are in Christ. Christ is in them. By the same token, the Spirit is in them, and they are in the Spirit. Believers dwell in and are in-dwelled, enveloping the Spirit who dwells in them even while they are enveloped by the Spirit in whom they have all blessings.

For Paul, this mutual indwelling of God and believer is a corporate reality. Those "who are many are one body in Christ" (Rom. 12:5), one body because of their common home in the incarnate Son. In Christ the gentiles who were outsiders, excluded strangers and aliens, have been drawn near, since Christ is "our peace" (Eph. 2:14). The body is one because it is animated by a single Spirit, the soul of the body of Christ, who equips every member of the body with the power to contribute to the common good (1 Cor. 12). The church is one with Christ because Christ and the church are filled with the same Spirit, the Spirit of the Father who is the Spirit of Sonship.[6] For Paul, the church's "housing" of Christ is not static. Christ takes up his dwelling in the church so that the church can "grow up" to be like the head (Eph. 4:15–16).

Paul doesn't use John's overtly "perichoretic" language about this body of the church. He doesn't say that believers are "one just as" the Father and Son are one. But he hints at a mutual indwelling of the members of those who are in Christ and the Spirit. Because they form a single body, the fortunes of each member of the body affect all the other members. One suffers, and all suffer. One rejoices, and the whole body rejoices. Each cares for every other, each honors every other, especially those members that are least honorable (1 Cor. 12:21–27). Their lives are entwined because they are each homes for Christ in the Spirit, and because all make their homes in Christ and the Spirit.

At times, Paul hints at a cosmic perichoresis. All things are summed up in Christ (Eph. 1:10), and Paul elaborates to emphasize that nothing is excluded: "things in the heavens and things on the earth." Heaven and earth are now at home in the incarnate Son of God, not just in general but also as a collection of "things." Stars, sea anemones, crickets and cricket pitches, London and Mumbai and Tianjin, parliament houses and the Jumeirah Beach Hotel in Dubai—it's all summed up in Christ. Christ is the atmosphere and context within which everything exists. He is the head not only over the church but also over all things (Eph. 1:23).

And vice versa, for Christ not only is the home for all but also makes his home everywhere in every thing, since he "fills all in all" (again, Eph. 1:23). The church is his body and temple, but Paul suggests that Jesus has also taken up residence in a cosmic temple. In Ephesians, this is a result of the exaltation of Christ, but elsewhere Paul hints further that the creation as such exists within God: "In Him we live and move and exist" (Acts 17:28). Creatures have existence only by God's gift of life and breath (Acts 17:25), only by virtue of their dependent relation with the Creator. But Paul goes a step further here, by specifying the shape this relationship takes. We live and are only as we are "in him," only as God makes room for us in himself. The world is nestled in God, and God intends to make the world a house and temple for himself. Everything in the world has a home in God, and God makes everything a home for himself.

The world has the shape it has because it is created by the Triune God, who is a community of mutual indwelling—because the God who creates is the Father who is in the Son by the Spirit, the Son who is in the Father by the Spirit, the Father who is in the Spirit, and the Son who occupies the Spirit along with the Father. The Triune God is in the world, nearer to us than we are to ourselves, yet the world is also encompassed by his loving presence. He *does* have the whole world in his hands, even while he inhabits the whole world. For Christians, being saved means being caught up into this communion, indwelled by God and indwelling him, and being opened up so that other people have room in us and we in them.

Every feature of creation that we have examined takes on a new brilliance when we recognize that both God and humans are in a relation of mutual habitation. The perichoretic patterns of creation offer fresh, biblically grounded ways to imagine God. God is in the world and the world in God, as I am in the world and the world in me. Creation resembles the Creator, and the human being as *imago Dei* is a created Son who resembles his Father. Sex physically expresses not only the indwelling of love but also the indwelling love of God for his bride, the creation, and the creation's union with her God. The Triune God indwells every moment of time with all that he is, and in that indwelling is simultaneously the God of all times. God inhabits the past as the God of present and future, the present as the Alpha and Omega, and the future as the God who has indwelled every past moment until the end of time. God has spoken, and his Word is in the world, even as the world is created and sustained by the Word. As the music of God, the Spirit inspires hearts to sing; the Spirit who hovered over the formless and empty waters harmonizes, orchestrates, and sets the rhythm for all things. As we discover the pattern of perichoresis, traces of the Trinity, everywhere, so more is disclosed of the Trinity whose traces they are.

All this explains why the Bible can use such a rich variety of images to describe the redemption of humanity from sin.

Salvation involves a mutual indwelling of human persons in God, and of human persons in one another, so that human communities become one "even as" the Father and Son are one. Salvation is the adoption of human beings as children of the Father, so that, like the eternal Son, the children of God begin to take on a family resemblance to their divine Parent. "I see his Father in him" is the highest compliment a Christian can receive. Ultimate salvation is depicted as a wedding feast, when the incarnate Son who indwells humanity comes to consummate his love by indwelling the church. Redemption is a new age, one in which future comes to be present, where the "powers of the age to come" are distributed by the Spirit. Salvation is the Pentecostal fact that the Spirit who inspires and exhales the Word has come to indwell human beings, so that our words are inspired by the Spirit of the Word. The Spirit who indwells inspires singing, an expression of God's dwelling in us, of us dwelling in God, and of believers indwelling one another. In the eternal praise of the new creation, we will become one mighty sound, like the mighty waters, like the voice of God himself. The Spirit breaks us open so we can host others within us; the Spirit expands us so that we can house multitudes; the Spirit drives us ahead so that we gladly, redemptively, take up residence where the Son dwelled, in the slums of human hearts. By the indwelling of the Spirit who is indwelled by the Father and Son, the darkness of our minds is dispersed and we begin to see the world through clear eyes. In each of these ways, the traces of the Trinity that are hardwired into the creation come into their fullness in our entry into new creation.

The rest is speculation. But the clues of Scripture encourage us to look, and having sought, we found. They are no more than traces, but these traces are the traces, fingerprints, and footprints of the God who is Trinity.

Postscript

I anticipate three main objections to the approach to trinitarian theology I have explored in this book: First, there will be objections to the notion that trinitarian relations can be compared to human relationships, or to relationships among inanimate objects and concepts, as I have done throughout this book. This will be linked to a more general suspicion of the tradition of *vestigia Trinitatis*, the notion that there are discernible trinitarian fingerprints in creation. Finally, some will object to the promiscuous use I make of the notion of perichoresis in particular, claiming that the concept should be used only of relations between the divine persons.

In the main, though, I anticipate that these objections will not come from trinitarian theology itself. Rather, they will be "meta-trinitarian" objections, methodological objections, objections rooted less in trinitarian theology than in the theology of creation and the implicit notion of theological language. It is my conviction that most of the debates about trinitarian theology today are of this sort, so addressing those underlying or overarching presuppositions will be the focus of this postscript.

The category of "relation" has long been central to trinitarian theology,[1] but in recent theology the category has become a transcendental category, the leading feature not only of divine life but also of created life.[2] Human beings made in the image of the Triune God are analogically "relational" beings, and relationality is said to characterize the nonhuman world as well.

Among the critics of this approach, Kathryn Tanner and Lewis Ayres stand out for their clarity. Since God and humans are different, the move from talk of God's relationality to human relationships is not, Tanner insists, straightforward. Because of the gap between God and human beings, ordinary language does not apply to God in the same way it does to humans. What does "equal" mean in the statement "divine persons are equal"? What do "person" or "relation" mean when applied to God? Divine persons *are* their relations, but human beings exist, Tanner says, before the relations they have among themselves. Further, divine persons have a fixed relationality that is not characteristic of human beings: the Father is no one's Son, and the Son will never be a Father.[3] Ayres likewise objects that attempts at trinitarian ontology are unclear about their concept of analogy. A proper concept of analogy must both honor the Creator-creature distinction and recognize the presence of God within his creation. Because of the differences between God and humans, terms like "relation" cannot be used univocally when applied to one or the other. Ayres is also concerned that relational ontologies bypass the classical emphasis on contemplative purification, involving both meditation on Scripture, with attention to the unfolding revelation of Scripture, as well as participation in the life of the church. Relational ontologies too often treat trinitarian patterns of life as if they were blueprints that could be grasped by just anyone and applied to some human grouping.[4]

Princeton's Bruce McCormack brings similar protests against the "uncritical expansion of the concept of perichoresis today on the part of a good many theologians." Today, he complains, theologians promiscuously apply it in contexts where it doesn't fit: "We are suffering from 'creeping perichoresis.'" Strictly, the word describes the "purely spiritual relations" of the three persons, who all share one substance. It "is rightly employed in trinitarian discourse for describing that which is dissimilar in the analogy between intra-trinitarian relations among the divine 'persons' on the one hand and human to human relations on the other." Theologians abuse language and reality when they apply it to human relations, since human beings "remain distinct individuals even in the most intimate of their relations." To speak of the believer's relation with Jesus as "perichoretic" is also invalid, for Jesus and the believers are not absorbed into one entity.[5]

Before responding, I should note that both Tanner and Ayres believe that trinitarian theology, properly understood and used, *does* provide resources for understanding creation and human relationality. Tanner's concern is largely to emphasize God's initiative in restoring human relations. Humans do not imitate but *participate in* the divine communion. Thus she highlights the mission of the Son and Spirit. The relations of the divine persons in the economy of redemption affect human relations: "A life empowered by the Spirit in service to the mission of the Father for the world means that Jesus is with and for us, and that we, in turn, are to be with and for one another." Thus the mission does bring in a "new community" whose "way of being is what the Trinitarian relations as they show themselves in the economy . . . amount to in human relational terms."[6] Having made proper qualifications, Ayres too concludes that "the divine relationships certainly should provide material that should be of immense help in shaping our vision of the world" and can "serve as a guide for our engagement of ontological thought." Created things do reflect God, but we see that reflection rightly when "the grasping is part of our move towards the Creator."[7]

Still there are substantive problems with Tanner's and Ayres's objections. Specifically, Tanner fails to reckon with the import of the most important biblical passages. She cites Jesus's prayer that "they may be one as we are one" (John 17:11, 22) but concludes that this may only indicate "the centrality of Christ, and of his relations with the Father, for our relations with the Father."[8] She ignores the critical text (v. 21), where Jesus asks the Father with whom he is one by mutual indwelling that the disciples might be one "just as" (*kathōs*) "you, Father, *are* in Me and I in You." Tanner is correct to stress that the image of divine life among the disciples utterly depends on the missions of the Son and Spirit, by which the disciples share in the communion of Father, Son, and Spirit, and she is also correct to stress that the interpersonal relations expressed in the mission come, by the power of the Spirit, to characterize the life of believers. But she weakens Jesus's prayer concerning the result of this mission: that the common life of the disciples would come to bear the imprint of the eternal perichoretic relation of the Father and Son.

The more general problem with both Tanner and Ayres, and with many of their allies, lies in their implied notions of the Creator-creature distinction and of analogy. The objections arise, I submit, from a faulty doctrine of creation.

Scripture uses many words and names to portray God, his character, and his actions. Many of the descriptions of God are applications of created terms to God: God is Rock, Light, Sun, Shield, and so on. He stands in relation to humanity and Israel in ways describable in terms of human relations: he is King, Father, Lord, Husband.

Though the words must be taken in an analogical sense, Scripture exhibits no anxiety about using them. Nowhere in Scripture is there any hint that such analogies and figures are incapable of telling the truth about God, nor do we find any hint of the gymnastics typical of theological discussions of analogy (e.g., the common claim that God is infinitely *dissimilar* to whatever we compare him to). Scripture claims that many of these terms are God's own self-descriptions (e.g., Gen. 15:1), and naively supposes that human language can accurately reveal God. The import of these descriptions seems straightforward: God is rock-like and shieldlike, kinglike and fatherlike in some unspecified but meaningful way. *How* he is such is left to context and narrative. "Just as a father has compassion on his children, so the LORD has compassion on those who fear Him" (Ps. 103:13). More mysteriously, he is the Rock that begot Israel (Deut. 32).

The point here is not to expound these images, but merely to note their unproblematic presence everywhere in the Bible. That is simply a description of the phenomenon of Scripture. But it is a noteworthy phenomenon, and we should pause to ask how it is that Scripture is so very *un*concerned about the problems that have preoccupied theologians for many centuries. That demands some explanation.

Perhaps the biblical writers are theologically naive. They believe that ordinary human language can tell the truth about God, and that ordinary things in the world make suitable analogies to God. In particular, it may be that they were incapable of conceiving God's majesty and transcendence. That's implausible. The same Isaiah who trembles in awe before Yahweh's majesty describes him without embarrassment as a "Lord" (*adonai*) who sits on a throne wearing a robe (Isa. 6:1).

I suggest that the Bible is unselfconscious about its language because of the assumed view of creation and human nature, and therefore of human language.

All created things were made by God, designed after his Wisdom and Logos. As such, creation is communication from God about God (Ps. 19).[9] God made rocks, and in making them (we may surmise) intended them to display at least some radiance of his glory. God created human beings in his image, and in so doing designed them to be suitable icons of his character. God oversaw the formation of human families and polities, and as he did so, he directed them so that "fathers" and "kings" depict in various ways how Yahweh relates to his creation, to human beings, and to his people in particular. Ultimately, he designed the world so that fathers and sons would point toward the eternal Father who loves his eternal Son. God created everything to communicate of himself and providentially directs creation to the same end. If that is what created things *are*, and if God is the Creator who knows and governs his universe, then created things are *designed* to speak of him. There is no impropriety in calling God Rock, Sun, Father, or in suggesting that there are analogies between father-son relations and the eternal relation of the Father and Son. Though "Father, Son, and Spirit" is an unrevisable name, Scripture sometimes, for example, uses maternal analogies to describe God's relation to his people: "as one whom his mother comforts, so I will comfort you" (Isa. 66:13). There would seem to be no obstacle to extending these analogies, provided we recognize when we leave behind definite statements of Scripture and begin to speculate.

Scripture also assumes that God is capable of human speech. Because God has designed creation and humanity and ordinary human language to communicate about him, he can speak clearly in ordinary human language about himself. God has revealed himself in human language, that human language has been preserved in the Bible, and it is ordinary human language. Therefore, ordinary human language is adequate for communicating the reality of God to us. Of course, there is mystery at every point,[10] but why should we expect anything else? We want to talk about, and to, an infinite, incomprehensible God.

Many theologians don't take this at face value. Tanner begins her essay with questions about whether "ordinary language" is capable of describing God adequately. If we give a negative answer to that question, we face two options: either we must have access to some *extraordinary* language that *can* describe God adequately, or we are left in silence. Or, in practice, we let certain descriptions of God slip through, but catch others with our apophatic net. What determines what gets through and what doesn't is a question that charity prevents me from speculating about.

Of course, the biblical analogies must be handled with care. Of course, we must not conclude that, because we grasp something of how human beings relate, we know *exactly* what sort of relation the Father has with the Son. But we should be no more anxious about these analogies than Scripture is, and we should certainly not be so anxious about the limits of human knowledge and speech that we are reduced to silence. We worship a God who is Word; he has spoken, and he expects us to speak his words after him. He expects us to learn how to use *everything* he has revealed and named to honor, praise, and tell of him, because that is the destiny for which everything was created.

Notes

Preface

1. See John Frame, *Doctrine of God* (Phillipsburg, NJ: P&R, 2002), appendix A, for a list of over one hundred triads that may illumine or reflect the reality of the Trinity.

2. I have in mind Jürgen Moltmann, specifically.

3. Colin Gunton, Robert Jenson, John Milbank, and John Zizioulas have been the most formative for me.

Chapter 1 Outside In, Inside Out

1. This is one of Descartes's most important mistakes. I am not a seeing, experiencing thing inside the box of my body. It's my *body* doing the seeing and experiencing. Once we correct Descartes there, we have to re-envisage everything else too.

2. Maurice Merleau-Ponty, *Phenomenology of Perception* (London: Routledge, 1962), 82, quoted in James K. A. Smith, *Imagining the Kingdom: How Worship Works* (Grand Rapids: Baker, 2013), 44.

3. Merleau-Ponty, *Phenomenology of Perception*, xi–xii, quoted in Smith, *Imagining the Kingdom*, 42. Martin Heidegger coined his own German term to describe what we actually are. Human beings are *Dasein*, which means "Being-there." We are beings, but if we stop with that, we can easily think of ourselves as beings that float above the world or hide outside the world, or who can survey the world from a safe mental perch somewhere. We are not merely beings but beings who are always *there*, always somewhere, and we are surrounded by objects that already have their uses, uses we have to learn.

4. Cases of "inedia" are intriguing. See the 2010 report on Prahlad Jani, who claims to have gone seventy years without food or water and without urinating

or defecating. Tom Rawstorne, "The Man Who Says He Hasn't Eaten or Drunk for 70 Years: Why Are Eminent Doctors Taking Him Seriously?," *Mail Online*, May 8, 2010, http://www.dailymail.co.uk/news/article-1274779/The-man-says -eaten-drunk-70-years-Why-eminent-doctors-taking-seriously.html. Jani claims that he received his ability to live without normal sustenance from his devotion to the Hindu goddess Amba.

5. Rupert Sheldrake has explored alternative accounts of sight in *The Sense of Being Stared At* (New York: Random House, 2004). He claims that vision involves projections that extend beyond the brain and the body: "Projection takes place through perceptual fields, extending out beyond the brain, connecting the seeing animal with that which is seen. Vision is rooted in the activity of the brain, but is not confined to the inside of the head." Like magnetic fields, minds create perceptual fields (42–43). If Sheldrake is correct, then the thesis of this chapter is further strengthened.

6. Diane Ackerman, *A Natural History of the Senses* (New York: Random House, 2011), 10.

7. Philip Jenkins, *Laying Down the Sword: Why We Can't Ignore the Bible's Violent Verses* (San Francisco: HarperOne, 2012), 16–17. See Sergio Della Sala, ed., *Forgetting* (New York: Psychology Press, 2010); Viktor Mayer-Schonberger, *Delete* (Princeton: Princeton University Press, 2009).

8. Rupert Sheldrake, *The Science Delusion* (London: Coronet Books, 2012), 59.

9. Ibid., 61–62.

10. Karl Popper and John C. Eccles, *The Self and Its Brain: An Argument for Interactionism* (London: Routledge, 1984), quoted in Sheldrake, *Science Delusion*, 60–61.

11. Kelly Cline, "Solid Objects Are Mostly Empty Space," *Independent Record*, June 6, 2012, http://helenair.com/lifestyles/health-med-fit/solid-objects-are-mostly -empty-space/article_32b70fa2-af9f-11e1-8062-001a4bcf887a.html.

12. Robert Hughes, *The Shock of the New* (New York: Knopf, 1991), 17.

13. Bernard D'Espagnat, *The Conceptual Foundations of Quantum Mechanics* (Reading, MA: Benjamin, 1976), 286, quoted in Sheldrake, *Science Delusion*, 295.

14. That's not as spooky as it sounds. An electron is only detectable if we can get a photon to interact with it. But that photon changes the way the electron is moving. Because of our method of measurement, measurements affect the thing being measured when the thing is as tiny as an electron.

15. As Heidegger well knew, this insight was really a recovery of some of the central insights of ancient thought. Though Heidegger tended to look all the way back to the pre-Socratics, much of what he says about things has roots in Aristotle. For Aristotle, the "final cause" or "purpose" was one of the causes that made a thing what it is. In fact, for Aristotle, the final cause is the first cause: before you determine the materials or shape of a building, you consider what it will be used for. The final cause is a kind of "ready-to-hand" causation.

16. This is the illustration that Philipp W. Rosemann uses to explain the fundamental premises of Thomistic metaphysics. See *Omne ens est aliquid: Introduction à la lecture du 'systeme' philosophique de saint Thomas d'Aquin* (Louvain: Peeters, 1996), 49.

Chapter 2 Like Father, Like Son

1. J. H. van den Berg, *A Different Existence* (Pittsburgh: Duquesne University Press, 1972), quoted in Richard Stivers, *Shades of Loneliness: Pathologies of a Technological Society* (Lanham, MD: Rowman & Littlefield, 2004), 2.

2. *The Journals of Father Alexander Schmemann, 1973–1983* (Crestwood, NY: St. Vladimir's Seminary Press, 2000).

3. Thomas Hobbes, *Leviathan* (Cambridge: Cambridge University Press, 1996), 13. Why can't human beings just be sociable? Bees and ants do it, and they don't have the benefit of speech that can "signify to another what he thinks expedient for the common benefit." Humans can't just get along, Hobbes thinks, for several reasons: because we compete with one another for honor; because a bee's private interest is identical to its public interest; because ants lack reason and thus never protest against bad government; because, lacking speech, bees and ants also lack the capacity for deception; because animals are happy when at ease while men are "most troublesome" when comfortable. Above all, humans can't be like the bees and ants because "the agreement of these creatures is natural; that of man is by covenant only, which is artificial" (ibid., 17).

4. Ibid., 16.

5. John Locke, *Second Treatise on Civil Government* (Cambridge: Cambridge University Press, 1988), 2.4.

6. Ibid., 2.8.

7. Ibid., 7.77.

8. Ibid., 7.87.

9. Ibid., 8.99.

10. Edward C. Facey stated the point in blunt terms: "Man must have the right to consume the goods or trade them with whomever he pleases. The latter activity is done within the free market, within the framework of society which encompasses the entire complex of all individuals and their multitudinous exchanges. Society is nothing more than a means by which the individual members may gain their sought-for ends more easily" ("Conservatives or Individualists: Which Are We?," *New Individualist Review* 1, no. 2 [1961]: 24–25).

11. Thomas Hobbes, *On the Citizen* (Cambridge: Cambridge University Press, 1998), 8.1.

12. This entire discussion depends on John Milbank's *Theology and Social Theory: Beyond Secular Reason*, 2nd ed. (Oxford: Blackwell, 2006).

13. The main problem with such explanations is not that they are reductive, though they often are. The more basic problem is that the "social" realities sociologists use to explain other things can never be isolated in their pure forms. Religion, relations of power, cultural values, and other factors are "always already" there whenever we begin to talk about society. Douglas is right that there is a "fit" between grid-group dynamics and religious views, but that doesn't prove that the grid group is the causal factor. Perhaps a group is high group and low grid for *religious* reasons, rather than religious in a certain way for grid-group reasons. A medieval city is a political organization, but it takes the form that it does because of Christian values. Guilds and other corporate entities in a medieval town take the form they do because of Christianity. Economic activity in a medieval town is not merely economic activity, but is governed by ethical norms enforced by the

church. Is a medieval merchant engaged in economic or religious activity? The answer is both, and also neither.

14. Mary Douglas, *Natural Symbols: Explorations in Cosmology*, 3rd ed. (London: Routledge, 2003), chap. 4.

15. With surrogacy and other tampering with birth, this is no longer necessarily the case. There's even talk of artificial wombs, which would eliminate the founding intimacy we all have with our mothers. So far, these are ideas for science fiction novels and movies.

16. Slavoj Žižek, *Violence: Six Sideways Reflections* (New York: Picador, 2008), 142–43.

17. Martin Heidegger, *Being and Time*, trans. John Macquarrie (Oxford: Blackwell, 1962), sections 29, 83, quoted in James Mumford, *Ethics at the Beginning of Life: A Phenomenological Critique* (Oxford: Oxford University Press, 2013), 98.

18. For those who are severely mentally ill, the social world is very limited. They lack the full capacity to interact with others or to be interacted with, and so do not fully indwell the social world of which they are a part. Even so, individuals depend on a surrounding social reality, since the most psychically damaged have to be cared for.

19. Heidegger, *Being and Time*, sections 25, 152, 155, quoted in Mumford, *Ethics*, 101.

20. All I know of addictions and family therapy I have picked up from Rev. Richard Bledsoe. See his "The Dysfunctional Family of the Gadarene Madman," *Trinity House*, March 13, 2013, www.trinityhouseinstitute.com/the-dysfunctional-family -of-the-gadarene-madman/.

21. Christopher Titus turned his experience in a dysfunctional family into a comedy career. How many more comedians shared the same experiences?

22. As Jerrold Seigel expresses it, "It begins from the recognition that the existence of certain other people is closely tied to our own, and extends outward from there. This is why sympathy possesses so much power to mold our character: it is a kind of expansion of self-love toward others. Through it, the self provides the vehicle and the energy for engaging in social relations on the basis of which it constitutes itself as a stable and responsible agent. The passionate self that is the core of individual existence thus generates the energy to construct its own social being. Through its identification with others it internalizes features of their character, and makes those features the elements of personal identity" (*The Idea of the Self: Thought and Experience in Western Europe since the Seventeenth Century* [Cambridge: Cambridge University Press, 2005], 133).

23. David Hume, *A Treatise of Human Nature* (Oxford: Clarendon, 1888), 365.

24. Ibid., 316.

25. Jean-Jacques Rousseau, *Rousseau, Juge de Jean-Jacques* (London: Dodsley & Cadell, 1780), 12, quoted in Žižek, *Violence*, 91. Jacques Lacan made similar observations. Desire is always directed to another person; it is desire for the Other. Our desires are directed outside ourselves, and in desiring the Other, we don't just want to possess the Other but want the Other to love us in turn. Our desire for the Other is in part a desire to be desired. But it is also a desire that imitates the desire of the Other. We want what the Other wants. Behind Lacan stands Freud, who saw this rivalry as the Oedipal complex, a fundamental structure of family life.

26. Edwin Friedman, *A Failure of Nerve: Leadership in the Age of the Quick Fix* (New York: Seabury, 2007).

Chapter 3 I Am His, He Is Mine

1. The poems cited in this paragraph are as follows: Herrick, "The Vine"; Frost, "Putting in the Seed"; Donne, "The Flea"; Marvell, "To His Coy Mistress"; Blake, "Gnomic Verses"; and Shakesepare, *Othello* 1.1.127, phrase spoken by Iago.
2. Karl Barth, *Church Dogmatics* III/1, trans. Geoffrey W. Bromiley, ed. Geoffrey W. Bromiley and Thomas F. Torrance (London: T&T Clark, 1976).
3. "The Flowing Light of Divinity," quoted in Matthew Milliner, "Sex and Mysticism," *First Things*, September 19, 2007, http://www.firstthings.com/web-exclusives/2007/09/sex-and-mysticism.
4. *Songs of Kabir* (New York: Macmillan, 1916), 54.
5. Hermaphrodites blur the physical distinction of the sexes, and the fact that some are born with combined sexual organs is philosophically and theologically interesting. My focus in this chapter is on the typical physical differences between men and women.
6. This is what John Paul II called the "spousal meaning of the body" in *Man and Woman He Created Them: A Theology of the Body* (Boston: Pauline Books, 2006), 12.
7. Same-sex desire is, by definition, desire for the same. There is a built-in narcissism in a man's desire for another man, or a woman's for a woman. Same-sex contact is still physical union, as two become physically one, but it lacks the important feature of irreducible sexual difference that defines the sort of relationship we have been exploring. Though my intention is not to discuss sexual ethics here, this phenomenological difference is important for addressing the ethical question.
8. John Paul II, *Man and Woman He Created Them*.
9. This is a purely theoretical point, as I am informed by an anonymous reader that lion eroticism is of the wham-bam, drive-by variety, leaving little time for relaxed postcoital poeticism.
10. See the analysis of shame in Edward Welch, *Shame Interrupted: How God Lifts the Pain of Worthlessness and Rejection* (Greensboro, NC: New Growth Press, 2012).
11. I am borrowing the idea of an ongoing conversation from Peter L. Berger and Hansfried Kellner, "Marriage and the Construction of Reality," *Diogenes* 12 (1964): 1–24, to which I am indebted throughout these paragraphs.
12. See especially Robert Solomon, *About Love: Reinventing Romance for Our Time* (Indianapolis: Hackett, 2006).
13. Berger and Kellner, "Marriage," 12.
14. My argument is about ontology, not ethics or morality. If we were to extrapolate moral conclusions, though, we would soon realize that sex outside of a lifelong commitment is sex stripped of most of its point. A one-night stand, hooking up, doesn't signify mutual indwelling of lives; such encounters don't signify at all. They are in-significant.
15. Alter, afterword to Ariel Bloch and Chana Bloch, *The Song of Songs: The World's First Great Love Poem* (New York: Modern Library, 2006).
16. Berger and Kellner, "Marriage," 11–12.

17. Christos Yannaras, *Variations on the Song of Songs*, trans. Norman Russell (Brookline, MA: Holy Cross Orthodox Press, 2005), 4–5.
18. Ibid., 22.

Chapter 4 Presence of the Past

1. At the extreme, physical harm might raise questions about the identity of the self: if I suffered such serious brain damage that I lost my memory, could not recognize my wife or children, and had to relearn basic skills, it might be plausible to say that I lost my "self." In such a case, the continuity of my bodily existence is the slender basis on which we can still say that I remain "the same" person. What if virtually all my body parts are replaced—what if I have a heart and kidney transplant, an artificial hip and knees, prosthetic limbs and skin grafts? Here we can shift back to locating my continuing self in the psychological continuity. What if I am both brain-damaged *and* replace all my body parts? At that point, we either have to say that I am no longer the same person, or invoke some transcendent ground for my selfhood (e.g., I am the same person because I was created by God with a unique soul, or I am the same person because of the continuity in the way God regards me). In any case, these puzzles don't change my fundamental point, which is that the continuity of the person cannot be located in a stable, unchanging physical body, since the body is always changing and can change in substantial ways.
2. Robert Jenson, "The Triune God," in *Christian Dogmatics*, ed. Carl Braaten and Robert Jenson (Philadelphia: Fortress, 1984), 116.
3. Ibid.
4. Ibid., 117.
5. Ibid.
6. See Augustine, *Confessions*, book 11.
7. "Time," in *Augustine through the Ages*, ed. Allan Fitzgerald and John C. Cavadini (Grand Rapids: Eerdmans, 1999), 834. The essay goes to heroic lengths to refute the claim that Augustine subjectivizes time. I am not wholly convinced.
8. Several of the essays in Eugen Rosenstock-Huessy, *Rosenstock-Huessy Papers*, vol. 1 (Norwich, VT: Argo Books, 1981), address this question.
9. I can verify, here on November 15, 2013, that past me was right about the state of mind of future me.
10. It would be possible, I suppose, to conclude that time is an objective feature of reality but not experienced subjectively. That seems nearly nonsensical to me, and at the very least it doesn't come close to describing the real world and our experience of it. We might speculate too about a world where every moment is a fresh creation. It's not clear how that world would be recognizably different from the world we live in. But we can say that the experience of most humans is that the products and results of the past continue into the present. And the complications of explaining how we have memories are too great to make this a useful thesis. This is a time to unpack that razor and get to work with the trimming.

Chapter 5 Word in Word in World

1. This is the picture Jacques Derrida challenged in his various writings, and deconstruction arose from his opposition to the Platonic-Aristotelian notion that

there are two levels of signification. In its place, Derrida argued that even spoken language is "writing." All language, not just written, is always already errant, proliferating and diffusing beyond the control of the speaker.

2. This distinction depends on neglecting the physicality of sound.

3. Of course, documents are not the only form of evidence we have for ancient civilizations, but the documents we have are only marks on writing surfaces.

4. I'm referring to the title of J. L. Austin's seminal work in "speech-act theory," *How to Do Things with Words* (Oxford: Oxford University Press, 1965).

5. This point is brilliantly developed in various works of Eugen Rosenstock-Huessy.

6. Augustine knew this, and discusses it in *On the Trinity* 8. There, he asks what "mental word" is connected to the audible/visual syllables "Carthage," and answers that his mental image of Carthage is assembled from his memories of visiting Carthage in person. He also has a mental image of "Alexandria," even though he never visited that city, assembled from reliable testimony of people who have visited. That image is what he has in mind when he hears or uses the word "Alexandria." If he were able to show his mental picture, those who have visited Alexandria would likely say "That isn't it." This is part of Augustine's argument about how we identify a "just man" if we are not already just, and he moves past the point about Carthage and Alexandria. But it's worth highlighting that Augustine here admits that he has some fragmented knowledge of Alexandria from others' testimony—that is, from language.

7. Augustine is said to have said, "I write in order to learn." I have found no confirmation that he actually said that. If he did, he didn't recognize that it was a strong argument against his own views of language.

8. Here I'm following the criticisms of Augustine found in the early sections of Wittgenstein's *Philosophical Investigations*.

9. The philosopher who recognized this most clearly was J. G. Hamann, a long-neglected Enlightenment-era Christian who is enjoying a boomlet of attention. Hamann focused on language in response to the philosophy of his friend Kant. As he understood it, Kant was aiming to discover a pure form of reason that was not contaminated by the contingencies of history or culture. Kant's pure reason was reason that had escaped the confines of language. But Hamann recognized that this was impossible. Reason has a social dimension; we converse and argue to come to rational conclusions, and this conversation and argument requires the use of language. All languages are contingent formations, with a history, complexities, and "impurities." This is the only sort of language we know, and the dream of a pure language is an unrealizable one. The best introduction to Hamann is John R. Betz, *After Enlightenment: The Post-Secular Vision of J. G. Hamann* (Oxford: Wiley-Blackwell, 2008).

10. This is the starting premise of the structuralist linguistics developed by Ferdinand de Saussure.

11. The following paragraphs are indebted to Emile Benveniste's critique of Saussure in *Problems in General Linguistics* (Miami: University of Miami Press, 1973).

12. Ibid., 45–46.

13. Even at the origin, terms are often not entirely arbitrary. Some words are obviously onomatopoeic. Hummingbirds go "hum," and the sound bees make

really is something like "buzz." Linguists have also noted that even words that are not strictly onomatopoeic have sound qualities connected with the thing they name. A rock may not be rocky, but the sharp -*ck* sound seems appropriate to name something with sharp edges. The diphthong *fl*- is, across languages, associated with fast-moving things: flash, flip, flicker, flap, flop. *Sn*- is a nose-sound: sniff, sneeze, snout, snuff, snore, snooze, snuffle, snort, snicker. When people are shown arbitrary shapes and asked whether it is a "pling" or a "plung," they show a remarkable consistency. Shapes with sharp edges are "plings," whereas smoothly shaped things are "plungs." Vivian Cook writes that "vowels with high frequencies such as 'i' go with small size and sharpness. . . . Vowels with low frequencies such as 'u' go with large size and softness" (*Inside Language* [London: Routledge, 1997], 52).

14. A point emphasized by Walker Percy in his various writings on language, especially in *The Message in the Bottle: How Queer Man Is, How Queer Language Is, and What One Has to Do with the Other* (New York: Picador, 2000).

15. See George Lakoff and Mark Johnson, *Metaphors We Live By* (Chicago: University of Chicago Press, 2003).

16. Thomas Hardy, *Tess of the d'Urbervilles* (New York: Harper, 1920), 431.

17. And this sort of mutual indwelling isn't confined to literary texts. Other forms of art display similar features. There is an interpainturality and an inter-sculpturality and an interarchitecturality alongside intertextuality.

Chapter 6 Chords

1. Of course, visual technologies make spatially and temporally distant things available, but to see those distant things reproduced, we have to have a clear line of sight to the screen.

2. This is the starting point for Roger Scruton's meditations on music in *The Aesthetics of Music* (Oxford: Oxford University Press, 1999).

3. Scruton examines the ins and outs of describing sounds as "objects" in *Understanding Music: Philosophy and Interpretation* (London: Bloomsbury, 2009).

4. Jeremy Begbie, *Theology, Music and Time* (Cambridge: Cambridge University Press, 2000), 24.

5. Victor Zuckerkandl, *Sound and Symbol: Music and the External World* (Princeton: Princeton University Press, 1969), 137.

6. Ibid.

7. Plato, *Republic* 7.12 (trans. Henry Davis [New York: M. W. Dunne, 1901], 252).

8. Kepler calculated the proportions between the orbits of the planets and claimed that they corresponded to certain musical intervals.

9. Begbie, *Theology, Music and Time*.

10. Zuckerkandl, *Sound and Symbol*, 241–42.

11. Rowan Williams, *Open to Judgement: Sermons and Addresses* (London: Darton, Longman & Todd, 1994), 247.

12. Begbie, *Theology, Music and Time*, 89.

13. Stephen Guthrie, "Singing, in the Body and in the Spirit," *Journal of the Evangelical Theological Society* 46 (2003): 642.

14. Scruton, *Aesthetics of Music*, 338–39.

Chapter 7 Making Room

1. Here I'm endorsing the "perspectival" approach of theologian John Frame. See especially his *Doctrine of the Christian Life* (Phillipsburg, NJ: P&R, 2008).

2. What follows summarizes Gabriel Marcel's notion of "availability." Throughout this chapter, I am heavily reliant on Khaled Anatolios's splendid analysis of Marcel in "Divine *Disponibilité*: The Hypostatic Ethos of the Holy Spirit," *Pro Ecclesia* 12 (2003): 287–308. *Tolle lege*.

3. Ibid., 294.

4. Gabriel Marcel, *Homo Viator: Introduction to a Metaphysic of Hope*, trans. Emma Craufurd (New York: Harper, 1962), 23, quoted in Anatolios, "Divine *Disponibilité*," 294. Anatolios elaborates: "We can say that the movement of availability is what enables me to encounter unexpected and even seemingly inhospitable circumstances as not ultimately an intractable impediment to my flourishing, but to encounter these circumstances in hope and trust as a new 'dwelling place' for my person" (294).

5. Anatolios, "Divine *Disponibilité*," 293.

6. Ibid.

7. The phrase is Marcel's, from *Etre et Avoir, Journal Metaphysique* (Paris: Aubier, 1935), 99, quoted in Anatolios, "Divine *Disponibilité*," 294. Anatolios suggests that the prodigal son parable illustrates this principle, in that the father in the story makes himself available to both sons. He provocatively suggests that the parable as a whole provides an "anti-icon of trinitarian life." The Father is available fully to both sons, but they refuse to return that availability. The younger son demands his inheritance, while the older son clings to his sonship in a way that excludes his younger brother from participation. Anatolios doesn't pursue the stunning typology here: first, that the eternal Son did not see his sonship as something to be guarded with jealousy, but opened it up to all the adopted sons of God; second, that Israel is the older son, who refuses to share his filial position with his dead-and-risen brother; third, that Jesus is the true Israel, who does what Israel refused, and leads many sons to glory ("Divine *Disponibilité*," 295).

8. Anatolios, "Divine *Disponibilité*," 294.

9. Shakespeare, *Julius Caesar* 2.1.294–95.

10. Genetic engineering may eventually reduce the chance element of procreation, but in so doing it will weaken the ethical dimensions of parenting. It will reinforce our natural inclination to surround ourselves with people we like, people like us.

Chapter 8 The Supple Imagination

1. This example comes from Vern Poythress, *Symphonic Theology: The Validity of Multiple Perspectives in Theology* (Phillipsburg, NJ: P&R, 2001).

2. The notion that meaning arises from difference is the insight of Saussure's structuralism. The recognition that this implies that there is a trace of not-*x* in every *x* is the inaugural insight of deconstruction, a valuable theological and philosophical maneuver.

3. The same is true in Hebrew, where "man" is *ish* and "woman" *ishah*. The first words that came from a human being, Adam's love song to Eve, play on this similarity.

4. The arbitrariness of today's political divisions is worth noting. As far as political "theory" and policy are concerned, there is no simple division between liberal and conservative, but a complex range of options. Differences get exaggerated because they are *politically* useful. Democrats gain by characterizing Republicans in a certain way, and vice versa. Coalitions have to do, now as always, with power, though talk shows want you to believe that the debates are about ideas.

5. Economists have often imagined a simple primitive economy, like Robinson Crusoe's on his island. However they might be theoretically, these are imaginative constructs and do not reflect any known economy in the real world. Even in the most primitive tribe, production and distribution of goods is intertwined with customary practices that resemble law. For the presence of "law" in primitive societies, see Bronislaw Malinowski, *Crime and Custom in Savage Society* (New Brunswick, NJ: Transaction, 2013).

6. This was the style of argument used, for instance, in Charles Murray's *Losing Ground: American Social Policy, 1950–1980* (New York: Basic Books, 1994), which argued that poverty programs harmed the very people they intended to help. It was a groundbreaking book precisely because it was written by a conservative arguing from a "liberal" premise (that the test of a good society is its ability to raise the poor from poverty).

7. This formulation is suggested by John Frame in various places. See his "The Problem of Theological Paradox," Frame and Poythress website, http://www.frame-poythress.org/van-til-the-theologian/.

Chapter 9 I in Thee, Thou in Me

1. This is not the first theology I've offered in the book. As explained in the preface, the entire book is theology, an effort to glimpse the traces of the Triune God in creation.

2. A good summary is found in Verna Harrison, "Perichoresis in the Greek Fathers," *St. Vladimir's Theological Quarterly* 35 (1991): 53–65. Jürgen Moltmann, Colin Gunton, Leonardo Boff, and others make perichoresis one of the leading concepts in their trinitarian theologies.

3. Hilary, *On the Trinity* 3.1.

4. John of Damascus, *Exposition of the Orthodox Faith* 1.14.

5. John Donne, "A Litainie," in *John Donne: Selections from Divine Poems, Sermons, Devotions, and Prayers*, ed. John Booty (San Francisco: Paulist, 1990), 87.

6. This point is well made by Aidan Nichols, *Figuring Out the Church: Her Marks, and Her Masters* (San Francisco: Ignatius, 2013), 27–29.

Postscript

1. Augustine's refutation of Arian arguments turns on the introduction of the term "relation" alongside "substance" and "accident" (*On the Trinity* 5), and Thomas Aquinas describes the persons with the metaphysical novelty "subsistent relations."

2. This is stated most forthrightly in the title of John Zizioulas's *Being as Communion*.

3. Kathryn Tanner, "Social Trinitarianism and Its Critics," in *Rethinking Trinitarian Theology: Disputed Questions and Contemporary Issues in Trinitarian Theology*, ed. Robert J. Wozniak and Giulio Maspero (London: T&T Clark, 2012), 378–82.

4. Lewis Ayres, "(Mis)Adventures in Trinitarian Ontology," in *The Trinity and an Entangled World*, ed. John Polkinghorne (Grand Rapids: Eerdmans, 2010), 130–45.

5. Bruce McCormack, "What's at Stake in Current Debates over Justification? The Crisis of Protestantism in the West," in *Justification: What's at Stake in the Current Debates*, ed. Mark Husbands and Daniel J. Treier (Downers Grove, IL: InterVarsity, 2004), 111.

6. Tanner, "Social Trinitarianism," 382–85.

7. Ayres, "(Mis)Adventures," 143–45.

8. Tanner, "Social Trinitarianism," 384.

9. Hamann put it well: God speaks through the creature to the creature (Kenneth Haynes, ed., *Hamann: Writings on Philosophy and Language* [Cambridge: Cambridge University Press, 2007], 65).

10. Tanner's opening questions assume that "ordinary language" is perfectly capable of capturing and describing created things, but that is questionable. Do we know what we mean when we say "*human* person" or "*human* relation"?

13387278R00106

Printed in Poland
by Amazon Fulfillment
Poland Sp. z o.o., Wrocław